Working Mom's

SURVIVAL GUIDE

Paula Peters

PLAN YOUR LEAVE AND F THE BEST CH · CREATE YC FIND CLOTHES THAT FIT) · TAKE TIME · MANAGE BREASTFEEDING AND WORK

MATERNITY DULE · FIND DEPRESSION WORK (AND ATIONSHIP O GUILT

Adamsmedia
avon, massachusetts

Published by
Adams Media, a division of F+W Media, Inc.
57 Littlefield Street, Avon, MA 02322. U.S.A.
www.adamsmedia.com

ISBN-10: 1-60550-005-4
ISBN-13: 978-1-60550-005-8

Printed in the United States of America.

J I H G F E D C B A

Library of Congress Cataloging-in-Publication Data
is available from the publisher.

This publication is designed to provide accurate and authoritative information with
regard to the subject matter covered. It is sold with the understanding that the publisher is not engaged in rendering legal, accounting, or other professional advice.
If legal advice or other expert assistance is required, the services of a competent
professional person should be sought.
—From a *Declaration of Principles* jointly adopted by a Committee of the
American Bar Association and a Committee of Publishers and Associations

Many of the designations used by manufacturers and sellers to distinguish their
product are claimed as trademarks. Where those designations appear in this book
and Adams Media was aware of a trademark claim, the designations have been
printed with initial capital letters.

This book is available at quantity discounts for bulk purchases.
For information, please call 1-800-289-0963.

CONTENTS

ix   Introduction

1   Panel of Working Moms

PART 1: BEFORE BABY

CHAPTER 1

11   To Quit or Not to Quit?

CHAPTER 2

25   Maternity Leave and FMLA

CHAPTER 3

33   Negotiating a New Work Schedule

CHAPTER 4

45   Your Career Plan

CHAPTER 5

51   Planning Your Leave—and Return

CHAPTER 6

63   Planning Child Care

PART 2: AFTER THE BABY ARRIVES: DEALING AT WORK

CHAPTER 7

83   Missing Your Baby

CHAPTER 8

89   Catching Up at Work

CHAPTER 9

101   Breastfeeding and Work

CHAPTER 10

109   Sick Time and Doctor Appointments

PART 3: AFTER THE BABY ARRIVES: DEALING AT HOME

CHAPTER 11

123   Household Responsibilities

CHAPTER 12

141   Juggling Two Jobs—and a Family

CHAPTER 13

149   Stresses on Your Relationship

PART 4: CARING FOR YOURSELF

CHAPTER 14
161 Your Health

CHAPTER 15
175 Making Mommy Time

CHAPTER 16
183 The Decision to Change Jobs

CHAPTER 17
201 What If You Decide to Stay Home?

205 A Final Note to You, the Working Mother
207 Resources
209 Index

Acknowledgments

This book is dedicated to all of the working mothers out there who do incredible things every day—and rarely get thanked for their efforts. You are at the heart of our great nation today, and I am so glad you do the work that you do!

I am very grateful to Chelsea King and the staff at Adams Media for envisioning this book and giving me the opportunity to write it. This book was a sheer pleasure for me to work on and a gift of my heart. Meredith O'Hayre, in particular, did a wonderful job of editing. I am also grateful to Mike Snell, who once again helped me put my best work forward, as the "midwife" of this project.

This book could not have been completed without the fabulous time and attention granted by my experts (all working mothers, too!): Lindsey, Teri, Lynne, and Kristen, as well as the excellent interviews with my working mommies (many of whom had to squeeze me in during lunchtime, after bedtime, or on the commute home from work): Sonya, April, Jen, Kendra, Christine, Lori, and Vonna.

And finally, to my family and friends, who cheered me on to complete this book during a very difficult year for me personally—especially my husband, Ryan, and my son, Zachary; my parents, Audrée and Dick; my brothers Joe and Jeff and their families; my husband's parents, Rich and Ann (and his grandparents Pauline and Richard); my Aunts Dee and Adrienne; my nanny, Brittany; and my best friends, Lisa and Michelle. Dad—we all miss you.

Many thanks to you all!

Introduction

I wish I had had this book when I was pregnant. If I did, I would have avoided many of the pitfalls and mistakes I made—both in my personal life and my work.

As a new mother, you will have so many demands placed on you. It is difficult to anticipate them if you don't know what to expect. There are the demands on your time, your marriage, your health, your psychological well-being, and even your career. This is a lot to balance.

Your best strategy for success is to be prepared for what is coming down the road. If you think through the big changes that you are facing before they happen, you'll be better equipped to deal with them.

There is no harder path in life than that of the working mother. There is also none more rewarding. You will laugh, you will cry, you will wipe up spit-up from your adorable baby, and you will thrill over your work achievements—all at the same time. And you will love it.

In fact, according to the Census Bureau, of the 4 million women who give birth each year in the United States, 51 percent of those who give birth to their *first* child return to work within four months. Some will be working full-time, some will be working part-time—in offices, factories, construction sites, military units, classrooms, and more.

I have been a working mommy since giving birth to my son, Zachary, who's now three. I understand your challenges and your joys. I can't say it's easy, but I can honestly tell you there have been more laughs and good days than tears and bad days.

If there is one thing I can tell you as you start on your journey, it's this: You *can* do it. Believe it or not, you will discover many new abilities and talents that will help you along the way—the ability to multitask, your love for your children, and your ongoing commitment to your career. Each of these is a valuable tool that you take with you to tackle the challenges ahead.

And remember: No matter what the challenge, no matter how stressful, you will not only survive, you'll even thrive. And later, you may even say, "Wow, that was fun. . . . I'd like to do that again!"

Panel of Working Moms

When I began work on this book, I knew that I wanted to hear from other working mothers who had different experiences than mine. I invited several different women with various backgrounds and work challenges to participate. I even found national experts who were working mothers themselves—and intimately understood those special challenges. Here is our panel of working moms, who were kind enough to share their expertise with me on how they solved their daily challenges. You will see their suggestions, ideas, and solutions sprinkled throughout the book, in the hope that their stories will inspire you to write your own answers . . . whatever those may be.

Meet the Experts

Dr. Teri Sullivan

Dr. Teri Says: *Some women feel like they need to get everything done. The best answer for this: Don't do it. Reduce your workload at home, and focus on relaxing instead.*

Dr. Teri is a clinical psychologist who specializes in helping women—especially mothers—adapt to the combined stresses of work and family. During her thirty-six years of practice, Dr. Teri has counseled more than 1,000 women on techniques available for handling work stress, coping with new parenthood, motherhood stress, and marital stress. She has pioneered many of her own creative approaches to help women manage the transition to motherhood. Dr. Teri received her Ph.D. in psychology from the University of Arizona. She is a member of the American Psychological Association and is listed in the National Register of Health Service Providers in Psychology. Dr. Teri is the working mom of Justin, now twenty-two and married.

Lynne Eisaguirre

Lynne Says: A big mistake new moms make is thinking that they'll make a decision, and that's the way it's going to be. I don't think that happens for many women. That first year is all about changes. Life throws you curves!

Lynne is a nationally renowned speaker, author, lawyer, and entrepreneur who specializes in human resource issues in the workplace. Lynne has delivered more than 5,000 seminars to corporate workers across the globe and is the author of *We Need to Talk: Tough Conversations with Your Employee, We Need to Talk: Tough Conversations with Your Boss, Stop Pissing Me Off! What to Do When the People You Work with Drive You Crazy*, and *The Power of a Good Fight: Embracing Conflict to Drive Productivity, Creativity, and Innovation*. She is regarded as an opinion leader in the field of human resources and strategic conflict management and has appeared on *CNN Headline News, ABC News*, Bloomberg TV, ESPN, and NBC's *Dateline*. She is also the founder of Workplaces That Work, a business that guides managers and executives through complex change with their employees. Her client list includes Coors, Harley-Davidson, Southwest Airlines, and Sun Microsystems. She is the working mom of fourteen-year-old twins, Nicholas and Elizabeth.

Dr. Kristen K. Stuppy

Dr. Kristen Says: You can't make kids do what you want them to do. When my son was two, he was in the mode of getting himself undressed every time I tried to dress him, which made it difficult to get to work on time. Kids are just kids.

Dr. Kristen is a pediatrician specializing in children of all ages—from infancy through teen years. During her career, she has helped thousands of children and their families cope with a wide variety of medical challenges. Dr. Kristen has served as chair of the Pediatric Department at Overland Park Regional Medical Center and Menorah Medical Center, as well as on the Physician Advisory Board at Children's Mercy South in Kansas City. She is the author of "New Protocol for Management of Hyperbilirubinemia in the Newborn Infant." Dr. Kristen received her doctor of medicine degree from the University of Missouri School of Medicine. She now works with Pediatric Partners, in Overland Park, Kansas. Dr. Kristen, who volunteers regularly in her community, is the working mom of nine-year-old Joe and six-year-old Sarah.

Lindsey O'Neil-Hill, CNM

Lindsey Says: *I thought I could do it all—clean the house, take care of the baby, have dinner on the table. But I was exhausted after six weeks. My girlfriend set me straight, "You don't have to do all this by yourself. That's why you have friends, family, a husband. You need to accept help from others." Things got easier once I decided I didn't have to be a superwoman.*

Lindsey is a certified nurse midwife (CNM) who has treated more than 1,000 women in her five years in practice. She serves as a clinical midwifery instructor for Vanderbilt University, from which she graduated with a master's degree in nursing. She is also a member of the American College of Nurse Midwives. Lindsey is the working mom of Jacob, now eight months old.

Meet The Mommies

Christine

Christine Says: *Motherhood—no matter when you enter into it, no matter what you have or don't have—is a challenge for everyone. It puts everyone on the same level, no matter how much money you make.*

Christine, twenty-nine, is mom to Tiajah, age thirteen, Viviana, age nine, Mia, age two, and new baby Ella. Since marrying her husband, Joe, three years ago, she has left work and transitioned to the role of stay-at-home mom. Christine is in the process of completing her four-year college degree in education and has dreams of one day going back to work to teach. Her husband, Joe, works full-time.

Vonna

Vonna Says: *It's always going to be hard to adjust, but you just learn how to multitask. I think women are better at multitasking. It's all "doable," you just need to take it one day at a time. If you need help, ask.*

Vonna, thirty-three, is mom to Ashlyn, five, Gavin, three, and Elena, nine months. She and her husband, Brian, are both nurses. While she works as a cardiac nurse specializing in heart transplants, her husband is a critical-care float nurse, working in rapid response situations, such as ICU.

Lori

Lori Says: *Don't be afraid to take your kids places—even though it's uncomfortable at first—because if they don't learn how to behave in public, then they'll be wild animals. Who cares about dirty looks?*

Lori, forty-four, is mom to John, age seven, and Addie, age four. She currently has her dream job, working full-time as a sales operations manager for an international computer company. Her husband, Kurt, works full-time for an environmental engineering firm. Lori aspires to take on an executive role in her company one day.

April

April Says: *Success has always been important to me—both as a mother and in my career. I love my child, and I also love receiving recognition at the workplace. For me, I knew I needed both to feel complete.*

April, thirty-four, is mom to Ty, age four and a half. She works full-time at an advertising agency, while her husband, Aaron, is a full-time deputy who regularly works the night shift. Recently promoted to account management supervisor, April continues to advance her career—even as she and her husband consider having more children.

Sonya

Sonya Says: *Being a working mother takes organization, and it takes recognition of when you need help—help from your children, help from your spouse, help from your job, and help from others.*

Sonya, forty-two, is mom to McKenna, age ten, and Kramer, age three. She works full-time as a learning consultant for a national health care technology firm. Her husband, Mike, also works full-time as a salesperson.

Jen

Jen Says: *Balance is important. Ask yourself: Is it really worth it to get stressed out over this? Or should I be doing something else—like loving and teaching my baby? That philosophy has really helped me to acclimate to the changes of being a new, working mother.*

Jen, twenty-six, is mom to Isabel, twenty-one months; her husband, Danny, works full-time as a carpenter. Jen enjoys working full-time in human resources for her mother's family-owned manufacturing business.

Kendra

Kendra Says: *I'm not really a laid-back person—I can be pretty uptight, but I've decided that I need to be laid-back with the baby. It goes against my type, but motherhood has really changed me!*

Kendra, twenty-nine, is mom to Maddox, age eighteen months. She works full-time in merchandising in the apparel department of a major retailer. She and her husband, Brody, have been married for three years, and both work full-time.

PART 1

Before Baby

CHAPTER 1

To Quit or Not to Quit?

Let's face it. It's the most critical question you will ask your-self during your pregnancy: "Should I quit? Or should I stay?" Would it be better to quit your job and stay at home with the baby? Or should you continue working?

When I was pregnant with Zack, my good friend and business advisor Malinda suggested I wait until after my maternity leave was over before making my decision on whether or not to stay home full-time I said to her, "But why? I love working."

Malinda explained that she had worked with many women grappling with the same issue, and they didn't really know how they felt until *after* the baby arrived.

Malinda was right. By waiting until Zack's arrival, I could think through the issue with a better idea of what it would be like, which helped me come to the right decision. And I could enjoy my time home with my newborn without having to wonder if I had made the right choice.

In my case, I decided to continue working. That turned out to be the right decision for me.

Of course, as is the case with many, your financial situation may not allow you to quit work. You may need to continue working, simply to pay the bills.

But if you do have the choice to leave your job or keep working, it can be a difficult decision. Your choice may depend on several different factors. Here are a few things to consider to help you arrive at your decision.

The Five Factors to Consider in Deciding Whether to Quit Work

While there are a lot of factors that may influence your own personal decision, here are the five "biggies" that apply to almost all women.

Number 1: Your Financial Situation

Can you afford to quit? If so, then it may be an option for you. The big challenge here is: How do you know if you can actually *afford* to quit?

The simplest way to do it is to make a list of your total household income—including your partner's, or any other contributing family members—and compare it to your total household expenses. You should do this two ways: In Scenario #1, you should tally it up as if you were still working. In Scenario #2, you'll want to tally it up as if you were no longer working. Can your income cover your expenses in either case?

Don't forget to include baby-related expenses such as child care, diapers, clothes, and formula. You may also need to make adjustments to your income in your post-baby work schedule. For example, if you know that your post-baby work schedule might include cutting back your hours or working fewer shifts, then you should show this in your total. If you have no idea as to what your post-baby schedule would be, then perhaps you could run a few different scenarios, including one in which you return to work full-time and one in which you return part-time.

Scenario 1: You Are Working

In the first scenario, once you jot down all of your expenses versus all of your income, you will see whether your income will be able to cover all of your expenses. Don't be surprised if you discover that you will not meet your future expenses with *all* of your current income.

Our Monthly Income and Expenses

Income	Expenses
Ellen: $3,500	Groceries: $400
Jeff: $2,750	Mortgage: $1,200
	Car payment: $525
	Phones: $130
	Utilities: $185
	Diapers, formula: $200
	Dog food and care: $100
	Day care: $800
	House stuff (lawn care, etc.): $120
	Gas: $200
	Home insurance: $160
	Internet: $60
	Date nights: $150
	Take-out food: $125
	Hair and nail care: $150
	Clothes: $75
	Jeff's golf: $30
	Beer and wine: $50
Total Income	**Total Expenses**
$6,250	**$4,460**

Scenario 2: You Are *Not* Working

Now write up the lists again, this time without your income. You'll also want to subtract some of the incidental expenses involved with work, such as gas, work clothes, and lunches. How does the picture look now? Can you still afford to cover all of your household expenses?

Our Monthly Income & Expenses Without Mom's Income

Income	Expenses
Jeff's monthly $2,750	Groceries: $400
	Mortgage: $1,200
	Car payment: $525
	Phones: $130
	Utilities, TV: $185
	Diapers, formula: $200
	Dog: $100
	House stuff (lawn, etc.): $120
	Gas: $200
	House insurance: $160
	Internet: $60
	Date nights: $150
	Take-out food: $125
	Hair and nails: $150
	Clothes: $75
	Jeff's golf: $30
	Beer, wine: $50
Total income	Total expenses
$2,750	$3, 660

Yikes! The couple in this example wouldn't be able to cover their expenses right now if the mother quit her job. However, if your scenario is similar, you could also consider reducing or reallocating household expenses.

Dr. Teri Sullivan, Ph.D., a clinical psychologist who specializes in women's issues, and who has treated thousands of women—many of them working mothers—says that she has seen a lot of women who have taken the downsizing approach, with great success. "I have seen several clients who have a house that's way too expensive, so they work all the time to make payments and have little time to enjoy family life. When they downsize, they are much happier."

Once you have your numbers down, sleep on it. Come back to it. Talk it over with your husband. You may find that after reviewing the numbers, the decision is pretty straightforward.

If You Are a Single Mom

If you're a single mom, the equation may be pretty simple—you need to work to pay the bills. In that case, this will be a pretty quick decision, unless you can find financial support to allow you to stay home with your baby. However, if you really want to spend more time with your baby, you could still try to rearrange your work schedule (such as to four ten-hour days), or reduce your expenses so that you need less income—and therefore need to work fewer hours.

There are also lots of agencies out there that are helping single mothers. Why not take advantage of them? Agencies provide everything from day care, to baby clothes, to diapers, meals, and housing. You don't have to use it forever—just while you most need it, in that first year after your baby is born.

Find out what's available in your area—both government and private—and call them. If you're too shy to call, then visit their website first. An hour's worth of research may pay off for you in a very big way.

One of our panel moms, Christine, twenty-nine, used state agencies to help her pay for both day care and housing and says that it was a great experience. She estimates that the two programs saved her hundreds of dollars over the years.

"I was fortunate in that housing subsidies exist where I live," she says. "I was especially thankful because if I had had to pay full rent, I never would have made it."

Here are a few suggestions to start your search for a state agency or association to assist you:

- The Department of Social Services for your state
- The United Way (*www.liveunited.org*)
- The Housing Authority
- Your Local Food Bank (*www.secondharvest.org*)
- The Office of Family Assistance (*www.acf.hhs.gov/programs/ofa*)

Find out if your state offers family assistance resources. Get on the Internet and find out as much as you can about the organization. Then make a few phone calls and *get help*. Remember, there are people out there who *love* to help new mothers—they've built their whole careers around it!

Number 2: Feelings after Your Baby Arrives

For many new moms with their first baby, the million-dollar question is: How will I feel after my baby comes? Will I still want to work?

The answer is: you won't really know until the baby comes. And it will be different for every woman. In Dr. Teri's experience, some people go to work and find out that they miss their baby much more than they imagined they would. Others think they don't want to return to work, then realize that staying home isn't for them.

In my case, by the end of my maternity leave I was both relieved and happy to go back to work. In fact, I have rarely enjoyed my work as much as in those first few months after my maternity leave. For the first time in my life, I actually had a good balance of work and family—the physical demands of caring for the baby allowed me to enjoy the mental tasks of work more, and vice versa. The two areas of my life were very complementary and balanced each other well.

Number 3: Medical Benefits

Are you the main provider of benefits in your household? If so, then leaving work may not be a good option for you—unless you can find an acceptable (and affordable!) substitute.

Remember, you are going to incur higher than normal medical expenses over the next year—not just for you, but also for the baby. After your many pregnancy visits and tests are done, you then have the delivery and postpartum visits, not to mention the many upcoming well-baby and sick-baby visits to the pediatrician.

If you are the type of person who rarely visits the doctor, then once you have your baby, you'll have a whole new appreciation for your medical benefits—because you will use them frequently during that first year. Of course, if your husband or partner is carrying the medical benefits, then this may not be a deciding factor for you.

Number 4: Your Enjoyment of Work

How do you feel about your job in general these days? Love it? Hate it?

Here's a clue: If you're already feeling pretty down about your job, then staying home with your baby is going to look like a pretty attractive option—and that's perfectly normal. But if you're enjoying your work, you may be more motivated to stick with your job.

If you are really unhappy with your job, then be aware that it may not be a reason to quit altogether and stay home. Rather, you may still be interested in work—just a different job. So don't let your unhappiness with your job prevent you from doing satisfying work that you love (in that case, see Chapter 16, The Decision to Change Jobs).

Number 5: Stress at Home

If you and your husband both work stressful jobs already, then it is only going to become more heightened once the baby arrives. For example, if you are both routinely working fifty- or sixty-hour weeks, alternating twenty-four-hour shifts, or travel assignments, then what is now a challenging situation may get downright hellish once you add a baby, child care, and postpartum emotions to the mix.

With one person at home, there is someone to relieve the burden of doing chores, planning meals, going grocery shopping, and taking the baby in for doctor visits. This may actually help you *save* money in the end if you decide that the cost of child care will end up taking a large portion of one person's paycheck anyway.

Of course, you don't necessarily have to be the one staying home if your husband or partner is interested and willing.

What If I'm Still Not Sure?

If you have reviewed all the factors, and you are still not sure what you want to do, then my advice to you is the same advice that my friend Malinda gave to me: Wait until *after* the baby arrives *and* you return to work following your maternity leave before making your decision.

So go back to work after your maternity leave. Try it out for a few weeks. See how you like it. You'll know pretty quickly if this will work out for you. And if worse comes to worst, and things aren't working for you, you can always quit.

But if you at least reserve the right to make your decision later, you will feel less anxiety and stress over the whole decision-making process. And that's better for everybody!

The One Factor You Should *Not* Consider: Guilt

The one factor you should *not* use to guide your decision is guilt. So many women say, "I feel so guilty. I enjoy my work, but I feel like I should be at home with my son more." Or, "I'm afraid that if I'm not a stay-at-home mom, my kids are not getting good care, and they're going to grow up to be juvenile delinquents." I have also met women who feel guilty for staying home, and start to think they aren't doing anything with their life or that they'll never make any progress with their career. If you start to succumb to these thoughts, remember: Guilt is nonproductive. Guilt will not help you make the right decision. Guilt is just a way to beat yourself up.

There is no evidence whatsoever that working mothers grow up to have dysfunctional children. In fact, it's a silly myth that mothers harm their children by working.

According to a 2006 study by Adele E. and Allen W. Gottfried at California State University, no link exists between the employment of mothers and criminal activity of their offspring, no matter whether the mom's employment was full-time, part-time, or sporadic.

In fact, some research has found several *benefits* to families with working mothers. Children with mothers in recent or long-term employment were actually in better health than those with mothers who were unemployed for two years or longer. Fathers became more involved with their children, a pattern that continued into the late teen years once it was established. Work is also an important source of self-esteem, enjoyment, and self-reliance for moms, minimizing depression.

So whatever the factors are in your personal decision—don't let guilt be one of them. The bottom line is that your working will not effect how your child will turn out.

A Few Tips for Making the Big Decision

Now that you've thought through the issues, is there anything else that you can use to help you make your decision? Sure. Here are a few techniques that I have used with great success in making major decisions. If you feel stumped, try one of these.

List the Pros and Cons

That's right, sometimes nothing works better than a good, old-fashioned list of pros and cons. Start with two columns— one for work, one for staying home.

Take out a piece of paper and fold it in half to make the two columns. On one side, write down everything you can think of that's good about staying at work. On the other side, write down everything you can think of that's bad about staying at work. Then add up your total on each side.

Pros	Cons
Enjoy my work	Miss my baby
I like my boss and coworkers	Less income to pay bills
Get a break from the baby	Have to find day care
Working on a fun project due in March	
My career is finally taking off! I want to keep going.	
5 Pros	3 Cons

Which one wins? Your heart may already know the answer before you even tally the numbers.

Write Out Your Feelings

Do you keep a journal? If you like to write, then pull out a notebook and spend thirty minutes (or write for three pages, whichever comes first) writing about your decision.

Write down anything that comes to mind. It does not have to be structured, and it does not have to necessarily be about the topic of returning to work. You may be surprised at what comes up on the page. For example:

Wednesday, January 17

I'm really not sure what to do about work. Ryan thinks I should stay home if I want to. After all, how many opportunities will I get to be at home with my baby? Maybe this will be the only one that I have. But at the same time, I miss my job. I feel ready to go back. I wonder what my mom would say? Maybe I should call her.

There's so much to do if I go back, I can't even begin to think about it. Holy cow. I bet Sarah is still working in customer service, and that's a minus. God, I feel so fat. I can't even imagine fitting back into my work clothes. I'll probably have to buy a new wardrobe. It seems like there is so much to consider . . .

The answer may not be obvious as soon as you put the pen down. When you are done, sleep on the results. After you wake up, things may be clearer. If not, then wait a day or two and try journaling again.

Talk to a Girlfriend

Sometimes the best way to work things out in your mind is to share your scattered ideas with a close girlfriend. Something about the process of talking through the issue untwists your thinking. A trusted sister, your mother, or a cousin that you feel comfortable with works just as well. In the course of your discussion, you may even find yourself arguing one way or another—which tells you your answer.

_____

Not Now, Honey!

While you may be tempted to discuss this issue first with your husband, try talking to a girlfriend first. It sometimes helps to work out your ideas with someone who can relate to your feelings as a woman and a mother. Husbands are notoriously panicky about things like money and jobs, and that makes for a challenging conversation. You can always report back to him later about your thoughts.

Sleep on It

Sometimes there is just no way to force the right decision. After all, this is a very emotional decision, at a very critical time in your life.

If you have time available, then try walking away from it for one week. Just leave it alone—choose not to obsess about it. Sleep on it. Or maybe pray or meditate on it, whichever works best for you. Suddenly, when you are least expecting it, the right answer may suddenly come to you.

It Doesn't Have to Be One or the Other

The decision to work doesn't have to be all or nothing. These days, many companies are actively seeking employees who are more willing to work in nontraditional part-time or flextime arrangements.

If you enjoy your job (or need a certain amount of income) but don't want to return to the full forty-hour grind, then consider asking your manager to reduce your hours. At one of my previous jobs, I knew of two mothers who negotiated a unique job-sharing arrangement with their manager. Since they both performed similar jobs, and they both had children at around the same time, they simply worked the same job on different days of the week. It was a win for the manager, too, since they reduced costs for the company.

If your manager is not open to a new arrangement, then don't rule out the option of exploring a new job with an employer that would actually be excited to have a part-time employee. There are a lot of businesses out there that are delighted to work with part-time employees. For more information on negotiating a schedule with your boss see Chapter 3, Negotiating a New Work Schedule.

Ultimately, if you decide to work, then you'll need to know about the fundamentals—such as maternity leave. So even if you are undecided right now, be sure to read on to learn about your rights and challenges with this important topic—as well as the many other facets of being a working mom. Knowing more may help you to decide.

CHAPTER 2

Maternity Leave and FMLA

When it comes to maternity leave, the best approach is to educate yourself—and negotiate for what you want—as soon as you feel comfortable.

The first and most important step is to educate yourself about the laws in your state and the policies at your workplace.

You may be surprised to learn that there is no national maternity-leave policy, so every scenario will be different. You may be even more surprised to discover that maternity leave is usually unpaid. Let's start by exploring the five factors that affect your maternity leave.

How Maternity Leave Is Determined

There are five main factors that determine how much maternity leave you will get. They are:

1. Law
2. Your company's policy
3. Personal values

4. Your ability to negotiate
5. Your personal choice

The Law

As mentioned in the introduction to this chapter, there is no *federal* obligation to give women time off for pregnancy, delivery, or normal postpartum recovery. However, some states now have laws governing maternity leave. These state laws require companies to provide a minimum amount of leave time, either paid or unpaid. Companies can't provide *less* than the state dictates, but they can provide *more*. So be sure to educate yourself on your individual state laws—*before* you go in to talk with your boss or Human Resources department.

Don't Assume Your Boss Knows the Law!

Don't assume that your boss knows the law—or your company policy. Some managers are better at learning human resource policies than others; and some companies have not thought out their policies very well. Give yourself the advantage by educating yourself about company policy, the Family and Medical Leave Act (FMLA), and state law.

What about FMLA?

Many companies have adopted the Family and Medical Leave Act as their maternity leave policy. Although FMLA does not *officially* cover a *healthy* pregnancy and delivery—it was designed to provide unpaid time for an employee to care for herself or another family member with a serious health condition—it is now frequently being used *unofficially* to handle maternity leave for a normal pregnancy and delivery.

In other words, companies are not obligated by law to provide FMLA leave for a woman with a *normal* pregnancy and delivery. Although having a healthy infant at home is not considered a serious health issue, many companies are using it as a guideline for their own company policy.

More about FMLA

The Family and Medical Leave Act (FMLA) was created in 1993 to help employees take care of themselves (or another family member) when suffering from a "serious health condition." It offers employees up to twelve weeks of excused absence from their jobs each year. However, there are many strict requirements around FMLA, and the act itself is a complex legal entity that has been the subject of much debate and interpretation.

For example, FMLA leave is *unpaid* leave (unless your company offers pay). Moreover, to qualify for it, you must have worked at your company for more than twelve months before taking leave—for at least 1,250 hours in the previous year.

Not only that, but your company must employ fifty-plus employees within seventy-five miles of the employee's worksite to be eligible. In other words, smaller companies are not legally obligated to participate in FMLA at all.

There are many more requirements—so check out the following resources before approaching your manager or Human Resources department: *www.dol.gov/elaws/esa/fmla*; *The FMLA: Understanding the Family and Medical Leave Act*, by Will Aitchison; and *Your Rights under the FMLA*, by Margaret Jasper.

Regardless of whether or not your company uses FMLA as a guideline for maternity leave, you could still qualify for FMLA leave if a serious complication arose from your pregnancy, delivery, or postpartum recovery. For example, complications from a C-section, severe postpartum depression diagnosed by a doctor, or being put on bed rest during your pregnancy could qualify.

If there is no state law in your state, then you may be at the mercy of company policy. The bad news is that companies not governed by state law are not legally obligated to give you any maternity leave. The good news is that companies do it anyway. You can still rely on the other factors to help you out—including your manager's personal values, and your ability to negotiate.

Your Company's Policy

Your employer may choose to stick with providing the minimum level of maternity leave that your state requires—or they may choose to provide more benefits.

If your state does not have any law requiring maternity leave, then you are relying on company policy (as well as on their personal values and your ability to negotiate) to get your maternity leave.

For example, your company may have a written policy that states clearly, "Two weeks' paid maternity leave is to be offered to all employees." Or there may be no policy written anywhere—but you know that the last two women who gave birth while working there were given six weeks' unpaid time off. That would be considered an informal policy. Or perhaps you work in an office where no one has taken maternity leave before. In that case, you will be helping to create the policy.

The bottom line is, it's really up to your employer to decide how much time, pay, and benefits you receive during your maternity leave—above and beyond any applicable state laws. Talk to your Human Resources department (if you have one), ask your manager about what she knows, or speak to other moms at your office. Learn what your company has done in the past. Find out if there are any written policies. Educate yourself *before* you negotiate for what you want. (You can find more information about negotiating in the next chapter.)

What about Paternity Leave?

As companies increasingly recognize the important role that dads play with their babies, more and more companies are now offering paternity leave for new fathers. Some companies have been doing this informally for years, allowing dads to use vacation time—or offering additional paid (or unpaid) time off to be with the family. If your husband is interested, suggest that he ask his manager about it at work.

Personal Values

Don't just rely on company policy to determine your maternity leave. Keep in mind that many managers hold strong personal values about family and maternity leave, and they may lobby to give you more than is required by company policy.

This can work to your advantage. If your manager does not feel that the company policy is adequate, he or she may kick in some extras—such as pay, additional time off, benefits, or even an alternate work schedule when you return.

"Some employers value being family-friendly," says Lynne Eisaguirre, our nationally renowned panel expert on human resources and conflict management in the workplace. "Or they may really value *you* as an employee, so they may provide more than policy allows."

If you work at a very small company where your manager is the owner of the business, then you may be relying entirely on that person's personal values to determine your maternity leave. This can be scary—but may also work to your benefit. Be prepared to explain to your boss how taking the time off that you need will make you more productive when you return—and offer to compromise if your job is important to you. For example, offer to take phone calls and check e-mails at home so that you can get six weeks instead of two.

The bottom line is that in a case where there is no company policy and there is no state law governing the amount of maternity leave you get, then you are completely at the mercy of your manager's personal values. Some companies will not offer you any leave—and that's a challenging fact of life for many new moms. Of course, you can still try to negotiate a situation that's good for you. And you absolutely should.

Your Ability to Negotiate

Don't underestimate your ability to negotiate the maternity leave you want. Whether you are in a situation where your company has no maternity policy and no state legal obligation to provide one—or whether you are already receiving some leave but would like more (or pay, or continued benefits)—then ask for what you want.

The key is to take the initiative. Ask clearly and repeatedly for what you want. Think of it this way: If you want to take time off to spend with your baby, then you need to figure out how to do that while still helping your boss get what he or she wants.

Your Personal Choice

In the end, it also comes down to your personal choice. Regardless of whether you are offered FMLA standard maternity leave or a shorter, less desirable leave, you may decide that you need more time at home with your baby and decide to quit. Or, conversely, some women realize entirely on their own that they cannot afford to take off the eight weeks that the company offers and still perform their jobs effectively or meet their career goals so they voluntarily shorten their leave.

In any case, the goal is to know your state law, your company policy, your manager's values—and your own self. Do the best you can with whatever is available to you. Just remember not to sell yourself short—you may hurt yourself in the long run.

Be Prepared for Complications!

If you have complications in your pregnancy or delivery, be aware that you are going to need more time off. While this can undoubtedly impact your income, it's important to focus on healing—otherwise, it may take longer to get back to work. In my case, I started having contractions six weeks early, so my ob-gyn put me on restricted activity. It meant no travel and no outside meetings with clients—just taking it easy. As challenging as it was, it was better than the cost and heartache of delivering a premature baby, which would have happened if I had continued at my hectic pace.

Maternity Leave When *You* Are the Boss

Of course, if you are self-employed, or are the boss of your own company, you will still have to make some decisions regarding maternity leave. It can be *very* difficult for self-employed women to take time out for maternity leave. But it can still be done, and you should definitely do it, as much for your sanity and productivity as anything else.

Don't skip your maternity leave. Even if you think you can't possibly take any maternity leave at all due to the pressure of customer demands and lost income, it's always better to take some time off.

Look at it this way: You will be more productive more quickly when you return if you take the leave, even if only for a few weeks. It's always better to take that time with your baby. And the longer you can stay out, the more time you'll have to get things situated at home and with your infant, so you'll be in a better headspace to begin working when you return. After all, you would expect your pregnant customers to take a few weeks off. Why not you?

In my case, I had originally planned to take only two weeks off. In fact, on the night I first went into labor, I rushed into my office at 2 A.M. to finish writing the brochure I had promised to a client!

Big mistake. At the end of two weeks, I felt like I had been hit by a Mack truck. I felt exhausted, and utterly consumed by the challenge of learning this new job, the job of being a mommy. So I ended up staying out for five weeks.

I now recognize that five weeks was still not enough. Next time, if at all possible, I will take eight weeks off. Despite the loss of income as a business owner, I know I will ultimately be saner—and more helpful to my clients.

CHAPTER 3

Negotiating a New Work Schedule

Have you considered negotiating a new work schedule? If you think that an easier work schedule is impossible, think again.

Thousands of moms across the country have negotiated family-friendly work schedules within their current jobs—creating a winning situation for themselves, their babies, and, yes, even for their employers. These women have learned that the risk of negotiation has paid off well in terms of increased job satisfaction.

Why Negotiate a New Work Schedule?

You don't have to wait until after the baby is born to negotiate a new work schedule. If you already know you want to change your current work schedule, then you can even start planning for the change when you are pregnant.

If you explore the idea with your manager *before* your delivery, then you will go into your maternity leave with confidence knowing exactly what will happen to your work schedule afterward—saving you stress during those first critical weeks with the baby. If your manager denies your request to change your work schedule, then you can:

1. Try pitching the new work schedule idea again later, when your boss is in a better mood—or when the climate in your workplace has shifted
2. Find a new job with a more agreeable work schedule
3. Learn to live with the same schedule you have now

There are lots of reasons working moms choose to change their work schedules. The most popular ones include:

- More time at home with the baby
- Easier balance between family and work
- Less pressure at work to complete tasks

Of course, the number one benefit for most moms is the opportunity to spend more time with their babies while still actively participating in their jobs and careers. This alleviates some of the performance pressure on both sides—work and home—allowing you to enjoy each area of your life more fully. Many working mothers describe it as the best of both worlds.

What about you? Whatever your own personal reason, know that it will be worth the effort to restructure your work schedule. If you're not sure, you can always propose to do it on a trial basis. Ask your manager if you can try it for six months, until you can get into a stronger routine with the baby. That way, if it doesn't work out, you can always go back to full-time. Your boss would have to approve this, of course—but it may be a great way to explore a new option that will work better for both of you.

A Cardiac Nurse Goes Part-Time

Vonna is a thirty-three-year-old cardiac nurse with a very demanding job specializing in heart transplants, which requires a high level of focus and attention. This mother of three typically works three twelve-hour shifts each week, plus overtime and administrative work, acting as the chair of her hospital committee on quality. After giving birth to her daughter, Ashlyn, and her son, Gavin, she spent six months on part-time duty, working only twenty-four hours per week. "My boss was really flexible, and our hospital is really good about that," says Vonna. "Slowly, I started picking up extra shifts, after I felt comfortable."

Keep in mind, however, that alternate work arrangements are not for everyone. There are downsides. You may not be able to advance your career as quickly as you'd like if you are not available for choice projects or promotions; when you are not physically present as much, you may not be remembered when opportunities arise. Also, alternate work arrangements frequently involve a cut in pay or benefits, especially if you are moving from a full-time position to a part-time one.

Be aware that you may also encounter resistance from other employees who are jealous at what they perceive to be the special attention you are getting. And not everyone feels comfortable negotiating with their boss; in fact, if it makes you too uncomfortable to try it, then don't feel pressured to do it.

But if the benefits of being at home are more important to you, then it's worth a try.

Weigh the pros and cons, and decide what's best for you. Remember, you can always wait until after you return to work to see how you feel.

Popular Alternate Work Arrangements

The good news is that alternate work arrangements are growing in popularity. More and more companies are using them to entice good employees to stay.

After all, it benefits the company, too. It saves the productivity costs that come with an unhappy employee, as well as the more tangible costs (in time and money) of finding a new employee who is as well trained as you.

The more you can emphasize the advantages to your *employer* to allow you to pursue your chosen work arrangement, the more successful you'll be negotiating this type of situation. The following sections outline some of the more popular alternate work arrangements today.

Part-Time

Probably the most popular (and least complicated) work change is to continue doing your job but shift from full-time to part-time. Usually, this means reducing the total number of hours you currently work to some amount that is less than forty hours per week.

The number of hours you work is really up to you and your boss. If you currently work forty hours five days a week, then you may want to work thirty-two hours four days a week, or even twenty hours five days a week. Or maybe you'd really only like to work only one or two days a week.

On the other hand, if you are currently working sixty hours a week, then maybe forty hours will feel like a substantial break. All of these are legitimate part-time options.

The benefit to this arrangement is that you are working fewer hours, which takes some of the performance pressure off of you, both at work and at home. The downside is that you will likely be asked to take a cut in pay and benefits. It may take longer to reach your career goals. You may also end up being asked to do just as much work at the office as before—but in less time. If you are asked to do as much work as you did before, then it's time to address this with your boss. There are three main ways that you can address this:

- Ask to reassign some of your tasks (or shifts) to other team members
- Make your work more efficient—so you can complete all of the same major tasks during your workday, and skip the nonessential tasks
- Figure out a way to do some of your tasks from home

The best way is to reassign some of your tasks to other team members. Schedule a meeting with your manager and make a recommendation on how to complete the tasks you will be unable to complete in your part-time schedule. You may also want to recommend other team members who may be able to complete the work or shifts. Be aware, however, that delegating your tasks or shifts to others may cause some resentment on your team—so be prepared for the political fallout if you decide to pursue this.

Flextime

Flextime schedules have become increasingly popular over the last ten years. Flextime is a concept used not just by working mothers, but by all types of employees, in all types of industries.

There are many types of flextime available, but the two main flextime scenarios include:

- Condensing a forty-hour week into fewer days (such as four ten-hour days, or three twelve-hour days)

- Using a flexible start and stop time for your day (such as starting at 8:15 A.M. and leaving at 5:15 P.M. one day, then starting at 9:00 A.M. and leaving at 6:00 P.M. the next)

Another, less common scenario involves flip-flopping schedules of three days at work/four days off one week, then four days at work/three days off the following. For some companies, flextime may also mean working as many—or as few— hours as necessary to meet certain performance criteria.

Telecommuting

Telecommuting is a fancy name for working someplace besides the company office—whether that's at home, at a different office, at a hotel, or on the beach. For most people, this means working from home with a phone, computer, and Internet hookup.

This option is well suited for desk jobs, but less well suited for jobs that require your physical presence, such as plant work, construction, nursing, or teaching. However, even some of those jobs have an administrative component that can be performed at home or away from the office.

For example, our expert Dr. Kristen Stuppy struck a deal with her pediatrics practice so she could work from home for a certain number of hours each week. During that time, she catches up on her administrative tasks, without seeing patients.

Telecommuting is a wonderful way to bridge the gap between work and home, but don't expect to be able to watch your baby and work at the same time. I made that mistake when my baby was born. I thought, "I'll be able to work at home while Zack is sleeping—no problem!" I put him in a Moses basket on the floor, next to my computer. Unfortunately, he turned out to be louder—and less professional—than I had imagined. My clients didn't appreciate the sound of a crying baby during our phone calls, and it created a perception that I was not taking my work very seriously. Sometimes he even fell asleep on my arm, which prevented me from typing or moving around! I quickly realized I needed full-time day care, even if I did work from home.

As long as you have a sitter or day care, however, telecommuting is a good way to ease back into work. It can be done as little as one afternoon per week or as frequently as five days per week. Some working mothers even use telecommuting to catch up on extra work at home, after their children go to bed.

Lori, forty-two, works in sales operations for a large computer company with a progressive telecommuting policy. When she moved from the home office in San Francisco to Kansas City, she started telecommuting full-time from home, with the occasional travel to attend corporate meetings. She still does it today, while daughter Addie attends preschool and older son John is in elementary school.

Temporary / Seasonal Work

The nice thing about doing temporary work is that you are not locked in to doing a forty-hour-per-week job, week in and week out. You can gain flexibility, often without the envy or hostility of your peers. In fact, with temporary work, you can do your job for a few days, weeks, or months, when the company is the busiest—and often get paid more per hour than you did in your old job.

The challenge with temporary work is child care. How do you find someone who is willing to watch your child for only three days, or three weeks—and often on short notice? (See Chapter 6 for a complete look at child care options.)

If your employer regularly offers temporary or seasonal work, or you see a need for it at your company, then ask your boss how they would feel about you doing this. It may be a win-win for you and your manager. Just remember that if your current manager leaves, it may be difficult to continue this arrangement.

Job Sharing

One of the newest—and most intriguing—forms of alternate work arrangements is called job sharing. Job sharing is when two (or more) people split up one full-time job. They may each take twenty hours per week, or one may take fifteen hours while the other takes twenty-five hours. They share the duties equally—just at different times.

If you can work this out, you may discover that it works well for you and your manager. You could reduce your schedule, while your manager may discover that by reassigning a few tasks to less-busy office staff, she could trim two full-time jobs down to one. Be aware that if you job-share, you will likely take a pay cut. You may also lose your benefits (unless your company pays benefits to part-time employees).

Reduced Travel

Travel for a job can be a nightmare for a new mommy. Reduced travel simply means finding a way to do more meetings and work back at the office, instead of traveling to do the work in person. This may be for a short period—such as the first six months after you are back at the office, or while you are nursing—or it may be permanent.

Traveling less not only saves you time, but may also save the boss money on travel expenses—unless they have to send someone else in your place. The disadvantage is that if you make a permanent change, you may find that someone else at your office will now get any choice projects that involve travel.

Your Own Unique Solution

You are certainly not limited to the alternate work arrangements I've mentioned here. You may come up with your very own, unique solution that will work great. It may be a hybrid of two or more options (such as reduced travel and telecommuting one day per week), or it may be an entirely new way of working.

Be creative. Remember to sell it to your boss. After all, the company has to get *something* out of the deal!

How to Negotiate a New Schedule with Your Boss

The bottom line is this: Your company is not legally (or morally) obligated to provide alternate working arrangements for their employees who are new mothers. So there are no guarantees. Ultimately, you are dependent on:

• Company policy
• Company values
• Your manager
• Company history
• Your own negotiating skills

But don't be intimidated—it *is* possible to negotiate a new work schedule. Even if you don't feel confident that you have the skills to do it, it's worth a shot to ask. After all, what do you have to lose? If you don't get what you ask for, you'll just stick with your current job schedule.

For the maximum chance of success, Lynne recommends a four-step approach to negotiating a new schedule with your boss:

Step 1: Research Company Policy and History

"Educate yourself about what policies are standard at the company," Lynne says. "Find out what they've done for other employees." Inquire at your Human Resources department. Research the company intranet, if one is available. Ask to see a list of policies.

If your company has other employees doing part-time or seasonal work, then you'll have a better case for your own offer. Ask around, and find out if any of the other employees receive such benefits. But even if they don't, you should put together a plan and ask them. Maybe they have participated in such a program in the past or know of someone who has.

Step 2: Know What Your Boss Wants—Before You Meet with Him or Her

Is your boss passionate about cutting costs? Getting promoted? Selling a million widgets? Or meeting corporate objectives? If you align your request with your boss's personal goals, then you'll have a better chance of getting your dream schedule. Know exactly what you want to ask for *before* you schedule a meeting—as well as how this benefits your boss. Remember, this isn't all about what you want. You'll have to sell this idea to get your boss to buy it.

For example, if your boss is fanatical about cutting costs, and you want to move to part-time work three days per week, then point out that she will be able to pay you less—or perhaps no benefits. If you are looking to job-share, then point out that she will save money on extra phone lines, computers, and desk space.

The more benefits you can think of for your boss, the better chance you will have to sell your idea. Go in with a proposal that will help your boss get what she wants. If you can help your boss get what *she* wants, then *you'll* be able to get what you want.

Step 3: Ask for What You Want

Schedule a meeting with your boss, and ask directly for what you want. Tell her how it will benefit everyone—you, the boss, the company. Everyone likes a win-win. Then give her time to think about it afterward.

Step 4: Ask Again (and Again . . . and Again . . .)

If your boss says no, don't panic. Listen to what she says, and ask her why she's saying no. Get detailed feedback.

"Learn their objections, then go back and respond to those," Lynne says. Never consider the first no as a final decision. If they don't agree to what you want, adjust your ideas, taking into consideration the objections they presented, and ask again. Of course, if all else fails and you can't get the schedule you want with your current job, you can always look for a new job that will provide a better schedule.

CHAPTER 4

Your Career Plan

You don't have to abandon your career once you have a baby. In fact, many of the women I interviewed were actively working toward long-term, meaningful career goals.

Is your passion to get a degree? Work in a certain industry? Get promoted? Or simply stay with your current company for the next five years? There is no right answer here. The key is to know what *you* want, and keep your career goals simple and straightforward.

What *Is* a Career Plan?

A career plan is simply a goal or idea about the work you would like to be doing in the future. It may be a continuation of your current work in some fashion (e.g., "I want to still be working at this job that I enjoy in two years"), or it may involve totally different work that is new for you (e.g., "I want to leave my customer service position and move into teaching kindergarteners within five years").

Your goal can be as simple as one sentence or as complex as a list of milestones at different dates. But the bottom line is that it does not need to be written down, and it does not have to be complicated to be successful.

In fact, a one-sentence statement summarized the goals of most of the moms I spoke to. A few of these women had very concrete goals, while others had made smaller choices along the way. Some even avoided setting career goals altogether, preferring to go with the flow. But in every case, they made a *conscious* effort to nurture their career alongside their family, and they were happier for it.

Some of the women I spoke to became more focused *after* they had kids. For example, Lori's only career plan before she had a family was to somehow work in the technology industry. "I just wanted to work in the computer world," she says. Now, at age forty-four, with her two children, Addie and John, her career goals have become more focused. Currently, she is working in sales operations for a major computer company—which is where she wanted to be—and is now looking toward the future.

"Some day, I would like to reach the executive level at my company," Lori says, and adds that she is working informally with a mentor at her company to learn what she needs to accomplish this goal. Some of the mothers preferred to take smaller, incremental steps—without an overarching career goal. April, thirty-four, is an account supervisor at an advertising agency, and a great example of this less structured approach. "I take it one day at a time. For me, it doesn't happen quickly—it's a slow accumulation of new responsibilities."

When April's boss suggested that she take a promotion handling some higher-profile, more challenging accounts, she wanted it, but was afraid to say yes. Although she wanted to advance, she did not want to rush into new responsibilities with little Ty at home.

"I knew I could get in there and do the work, but I wasn't totally sure about what it would entail. I was afraid to commit. I was afraid of the extra stress."

Eventually, April took the promotion and performed very well. She was able to manage her time effectively to get the job done, and she and her husband were able to work together to accommodate some of the main challenges—such as her travel schedule.

Like Lori, April has informally adopted a role model at her office—a woman vice president who also has a son, just six months younger than her own. "I started watching her and how she was balancing it all. Knowing there was someone out there with the same struggles helped."

But a career plan may not be right for everyone. Listen to your instincts. For example, Lynne had no career plan whatsoever, preferring to roll with the punches. Her method also allowed her to have a very successful career.

Creating Your Own Career Plan

Your career plan does not have to be formal. Take a moment to think about it now (before the baby arrives, if possible). Ask yourself:

- Do I like my current job?
- Is there something I'd really like to do in the future?
- Where would I like to be in five years?

Your goal is to come up with a one-sentence summary that captures your career goal, and can easily be remembered (or posted on the wall). For example:

- I would like to continue working in my current job for the next two years.
- I would like to finish my degree in nursing by 2012.

- I would like to get promoted to supervisor by next December.
- I would like to be able to train other employees to do my job in the next six months.

Now you try it. What is your passion at work? Where would you like to go? Or are you happy right where you are?

Think about it, then write it down. Use this sentence format, like in the above examples:

I would like to _____ for/by_____ .

When you are finished, post it somewhere that you will see it from time to time—your bathroom mirror, inside your closet, or in your underwear drawer. As the months go by, you will see it and gently be reminded of your goal.

You can also decide when it's time to change it. For example, if six months later you are now training other employees, you will be ready for a new goal. Perhaps you're now interested in becoming a supervisor. Your goals will change over time—and that's okay.

The point is, children do not need to prevent you from attaining your goals. While they may slow you down a little, if you can stay focused on what you want, you can stay on track mentally and physically, especially during that challenging first year.

For Christine, her longtime goal is to get her four-year degree in elementary education, a goal she has worked toward as she has cared for her three daughters. Now pregnant with her fourth, she was only in high school when she delivered her first daughter, Tiajah. However, she persevered and was able to complete her high school degree and enroll in college full-time by the time her second daughter, Viviana, was born. For the moment, she is enjoying some time as a stay-at-home mom before returning to the workplace full-time. "I know I'll go back to school one day soon, but for right now, this is the right choice for me."

For other women who are enjoying their current jobs, the goal may be as simple as to stay in their current position for a period of time. This was the case for our panel mom Sonya after she gave birth to her first daughter, McKenna, at age thirty-two. At the time, she was working as a regional training manager for a large bank.

"I knew I wanted to stay in the field I was in, and I loved the stability of the insurance and the job; at the time, my husband was in a commission job," she says.

Today, Sonya is forty-two and now has a new toddler, daughter Kramer, at home. She still works in the training field but has made several changes over the years to get to her current job as a learning consultant for a health care technology company. Today, her career goals are modest.

"My only real goal is to have a respectable career in something I enjoy and to be a good role model to my daughters."

Sharing with Your Boss

If you are comfortable with your boss, and have a good relationship with him, then you may want to consider sharing your career plan if it involves growing within your current company. You can do this either before or after your maternity leave. This shows that you are serious about your work, and that you are in it for the long haul. "For working mothers, there is frequently a perception that you are not as dedicated to your job," Lynne says. "People feel they can't rely on you, or that you won't put your time in." Creating—and sharing—a career plan can help change that perception, even if you are only sharing it informally.

No matter what your individual career goals are, just remember to take it easy on yourself. The first year is the toughest—you'll have a lot of competing demands on your time and attention. And just when you think you have it all figured out, your family's needs will change. The trick is to be patient. Don't get frustrated with yourself if you find yourself needing more time for yourself, the family, or the baby. Once you get into a routine, you'll be able to refocus on your work and your career goals.

CHAPTER 5

Planning Your Leave— and Return

Before your water breaks, give some thought to how you will handle your maternity leave—and your return back to work. Who will cover for you while you are gone? How will you keep in touch? Taking the time to make a short, one-page action plan will help you make the transition more smoothly.

Why make an action plan? For one thing, it shows your manager—and your peers—that you are serious about your work. That gives them confidence that you will indeed return—and continue to be an important, contributing member of the team.

Shouldn't My Manager Handle This for Me?

Of course, your manager should be involved in planning your leave. Many new moms will be lucky enough that their managers will already plan this for them. But even so, you still demonstrate your high level of commitment to the job by taking the initiative to start the conversation and show your manager your plan, which is sure to score you some points.

Not only will your plan help reassure other members of your team, but it will also help you to think through the issues involved with your work tasks, as well as how these tasks will be accomplished while you are gone. You can relax more fully during your leave knowing that your tasks are covered, and you'll be able to get up to speed more quickly once you return. Basically, you will feel less out of it after missing several weeks' or months' worth of new assignments, job duties, and office politics.

When Should You Begin Your Planning?

The best time to finalize your plan is about one to two months *before* your due date. This way, if you do deliver your baby early for any reason, you will go to the hospital prepared—and relaxed about work. You won't need to worry about that last project you were trying to wrap up.

At the same time, one or two months is close enough to your due date that you will have a good handle on the current environment at your workplace, as well as all the tasks you will likely need to cover while you are gone. If you start planning too far out (say, three to four months), your job may change too much for the plan to have any value, and you'll end up needing to rewrite it anyway.

What Should You Include in Your Plan?

Your plan should be short. One page (or less) works best, but yours can be longer if you have more complex job responsibilities.

Your plan should answer the following questions:

- Your estimated leave date
- Your planned return date

- All of your major work tasks, and who will cover each one while you are gone
- Any cross-training required to help your coworkers learn your job tasks
- Your availability while out, by phone, e-mail, or pager (if any)
- How often you will check in while you are gone, and with whom (if applicable)

Don't be afraid to tailor your plan to fit your individual job and your needs. Throw in whatever you think is appropriate. If shift coverage is critical for your job, then talk about that. If you use certain procedure manuals or customer databases, then you might want to reference that, too.

It's Okay to Say No!

If you really don't want to check in while you're out, then don't offer it. If your manager *really* needs you to check in, she'll ask. After all, this is *your* plan, so offer what you really want first. You can always negotiate from there later.

Reviewing Your Plan with Your Manager

When you are done with your plan, schedule a meeting with your manager to review it. If you can do this at least one month before your delivery date, all the better—since that will give both of you time to make changes to the plan and ensure that all of your job duties and shifts are covered in the event you must leave early.

Send your manager a copy of the plan in advance and ask her for a short meeting to review it together. That gives your manager a chance to review your plan beforehand.

During your meeting, talk briefly about the key points of your plan: who would cover your job duties, how you propose to reassign your tasks, and any cross-training that needs to happen. Tell her how you'd like to stay in touch while you're gone (but only if you want to).

Then invite your manager to give you feedback on the plan. What changes would she like to see? Depending on your plan, she may very well approve the entire plan. But if she asks for changes, then revise it.

Also, if you need any help executing your plan, then now is the time to ask for it. For example, if you need to find time in a coworker's schedule to do some cross-training, then let your manager know. She may get a faster response than you will working peer-to-peer.

End your meeting on a positive note. Take this opportunity to thank her for your maternity leave, and let her know that you are excited about returning. Showing appreciation to your manager is one way that you can become a greater asset to her team—and that will inspire confidence that you are willing and capable to get the job done.

Remember that while taking maternity leave may be your right, it still causes a lot of stress and anxiety for the people who work around you. Be sensitive to that. Be grateful. And say "Thank you" as often as possible—whether you enjoy your job or not. An attitude of gratitude will make your transition much smoother, for you and everyone else on your work team.

My Managerial Experience

When working as a manager at a technology company, I experienced firsthand how busy a manager can be. Whenever an employee needed a leave of absence for medical, maternity, or family reasons, it threw our whole schedule into chaos. When an employee took the initiative to plan out their job coverage for me, I greatly appreciated it. Since they took a load of worry off my plate, I was more likely to grant their wishes for how they wanted to handle it. It was much easier for me to approve of someone else's solution for a challenging situation than to try to come up with a solution myself—because I had so little time to do it. So help your manager out. By doing this, she will be more likely to help you out.

Preparing Your Thirty-Second Sound Bite

As you transition into your maternity leave (and beyond), you will also want to leave your coworkers with a feeling of confidence that you'll return—and that you'll be as good of an employee as you have been over the past several years.

In this case, I extend the term coworkers to include customers, vendors, or other people you deal with in the course of your job.

In order to assure your coworkers about your plan to return, you will need to think carefully about what you are going to tell them about your departure. Before you leave, you will probably get a lot of questions from other employees, such as "So . . . are you taking maternity leave?" Or even, "What are you planning to do after your maternity leave?" In reality, they may be wondering if you will ever return, and if you do return, will you be as dependable as you are now?

Coming up with a standard answer—a thirty-second sound bite—will help you deal with these questions in a positive, effective manner. It will also help reduce speculation (and gossip) among your coworkers and possibly any political wrangling for your job duties.

More importantly, if you do plan to return, it will show people that you take your job seriously. This will ease your transition back into the workplace, and will calm coworkers who are thinking that you will want to "jump ship" as soon as the baby is born.

To do this, you will want to give everyone a standard, one- or two-line statement that you have prepared in advance (much like a politician might). It should be:

- Positive
- Confident
- Focused on the future

By being positive, confident, and focused on your future at work, you will inspire trust that people can rely on you to get the job done when you return. You do not need to give a lot of details about your leave if you don't want to. Those details are nobody's business but yours and your direct manager's (and possibly Human Resources). But you do want to be honest and straightforward.

Even if you are not yet sure about what you will do after the baby is born—let's say you are still considering the possibility that you might later decide to quit, and stay home with the baby—it's still important to project a positive air of confidence. After all, if you do decide to stay, you don't want people to feel a lack of trust in you!

If You're Definitely Coming Back to Work

If you already know that you're definitely coming back to work, then your goal is to simply reassure coworkers that *yes, you will return.* Answer those questions positively and honestly, without giving away too much information. Here are a few examples:

- I'm excited about getting back to work after I have the baby, so we can continue working together.
- I'm planning to take the same shifts that I am now, so as soon as I get back to work, I'll be seeing you regularly again.
- I'm only taking a few weeks (or months, or whatever your situation is) off, and then after that it's business as usual.

Try one out. See what works best for you. Tailor one of these thirty-second sound bites to fit your personality and your individual circumstances. Remember, the goal is to signal confidence, so that others will be assured of your commitment. When you start getting flooded with questions from coworkers, customers, or vendors, you'll be glad you did it.

If You're Not Sure Whether You'll Come Back to Work

Even if you're not certain that you'll want to stay at your job after your maternity leave, it's better to project an air of confidence about your work and your future. This will reduce pressure on you to share your personal decision with others and will reserve your right to wait to make your decision.

While you don't want to be dishonest, you aren't obligated to give too much information, either. Stick to a statement that's positive, confident, and focused on the future—without getting into too many details about your uncertainty or your decision.

Besides, if you do return to work, you want to make sure that people are not going to be uneasy about how long it will last. You don't want them constantly thinking that you are going to bail at any time. That will hurt your productivity, too.

You can deflect unwanted questions with a short, sweet sound bite such as:

- I'm excited about getting to spend some time with the baby, and I'm scheduled to be back in the office after four weeks.
- I'll be taking seven weeks' maternity leave.
- I'm planning to be back in mid-August. My husband and I are looking forward to having some time with the baby.
- I love my job, and I'm also looking forward to spending some time with my family.

See? You're not lying, but you're not saying one way or the other whether you'll come back. You're simply saying that you are, at this time, *planning* to return. You still reserve the right to change your mind, without getting into an awkward discussion about it.

Here's what you *don't* want to say:

- I really don't know what I'm going to do. I still haven't decided.
- I feel torn between staying home and coming back to work. Guess I'll figure it out after the baby comes.

Do you see the difference? Both of these statements make the listener feel that you're probably out the door for sure.

Project an air of confidence and positive feelings about your work and your future, and you'll deflect unnecessary speculation about whether you'll perform at the same level after the arrival of your baby. It will be well worth it if you do decide to return later.

Planning Your Leave When You're Self-Employed

If you run your own business or are otherwise self-employed, one of the biggest challenges on maternity leave is coverage of your job duties. How do you handle the constant flow of business, customers, phone calls, and e-mails while you are gone?

If you are truly a one-woman shop, then you may simply need to shut your doors for a given period of time. If you do this, make sure to correctly set the expectations of your customers. Hang a sign on the door, post an outgoing phone message, or create an out-of-office reply message on your e-mail telling customers exactly when they can expect to hear back from you.

However, you also have other options. You can check your messages once a day, and at least respond to customer requests, letting them know you'll get back to them by a certain date.

If you have other people working at your business, then train one of them to cover your major job duties for you—or at least respond to the major customer requests. It's easy for them to say, "Paula is out on maternity leave until October second. May I help you in some way?"

If you don't have any staff to help you, and it's imperative that the business stay up and running while you are away, then find a trusted friend or family member who would be willing to help you out while you are on maternity leave—even if it's only a few hours a day. Don't expect to get free labor—offer to pay them fairly for their work.

Another option is to barter with another one-person business in your field. You cover for them, and they cover for you. Our dentist does this regularly, and it works quite well. Or you could hire someone from a temp firm. While it may cost you a few dollars in the short-run, it may be worth the long-term loss of customers.

No, You Can't Watch a Baby and Work at the Same Time!

In case you were considering it, it's impossible to watch a baby and work at the same time. Although babies do sleep a lot in the first two months, they also fuss, cry, eat, poop, spit up, and generally are distracting. Not only that, but customers who overhear a fussing baby in the background will not take you seriously. So I generally discourage new self-employed moms from bringing baby to work. Get child care instead.

Remember to Set Realistic Expectations of Yourself

It's going to take you awhile to get back on your feet. You won't be operating at 100 percent productivity for at least four weeks after your return, so plan for that. If you decide to take a shorter maternity leave (fewer than four weeks), realize that your ramp-up time will take even longer—more like six to eight weeks. Be patient with yourself, and set easy, achievable daily goals.

Customer Loss

Any business owner fears the loss of customers when she is sick, or having a baby. Losing customers is a business owner's worst nightmare.

Can it happen? Yes. Does it happen often? No. And secretly, among my mommy girlfriends who are also small business owners, we all agreed that any customer who would fire us because we were on maternity leave probably wasn't a customer worth having anyway.

If your absence will be obvious, explain to your regular customers what's happening. Be honest. Contact them in advance (if possible), especially if it has a major impact to their plans. Say, "I'm seven months pregnant, and I'm due on January thirty-first. Your project is important to me, and I would like to handle this by (insert date here). Does that work for your time frame?"

Then propose how you would like to handle it. Would you like to:

- Work harder now to finish it early?
- Assign it to someone else (either inside or outside of your business)?
- Bid it out to another supplier?
- Offer a different solution for getting it done?

Of course, if you're a retailer or restaurateur, you may simply have to shut your doors for a time after your delivery—unless you can get someone you trust to take over while you are gone. If you do need to shut down, then be sure to notify your customers. Hang a sign in the door notifying them of your estimated dates of closure, or send an e-mail . . . and don't forget to mention the happy occasion. Believe it or not, some customers may even like you better once they learn you're expecting! It's also a good excuse to get in touch with customers you haven't reached in a while.

Before leaving work, there is one more major thing you'll want to consider: child care. After all, you can't be a working mother without it. Read on for an in-depth discussion about child care, and how to find it.

CHAPTER 6

Planning Child Care

If you are going back to work, then there is no way around it—you are going to have to find child care for your new baby. More importantly, you are going to have to find child care that is willing to accept an infant. Not every child care provider will take newborns.

Unless you have a willing relative who is interested in providing full-time child care, or a husband who is planning to stay home with the baby all day long, then you are going to need to figure out a child care solution that will work for you.

Start soon. Many new moms don't realize that the most popular day care centers have a waiting list. Sonya says that she got on a wait list when she was only four weeks pregnant. "In our state, there is a ratio of only four infants to one provider for licensed day care. It's difficult to get infants placed in a good day care, especially if you have a baby with special needs."

How Much Does It Cost?

According to a report released by the National Association of Child Care Resource & Referral Agencies, fees in licensed centers can reach up to $10,920 per year for a 4-year-old child, and up to $14,647 for an infant. Home day care fees are slightly less expensive, reaching $9,002 for a 4-year-old child and $9,508 for an infant. For more information, visit *www.naccrra.org.*

There's No Reason to Feel Guilty about Using Child Care

Maybe you've read horror stories in the press: the evil mothers who drop their kids off at day care, then spend less than five minutes with their children every night. Their kids grow up to be rotten, lousy, selfish criminals. Right?

Wrong. The reality is: Children of working mothers grow up to be normal, successful kids. Dr. Teri says that children do fine in good-quality child care, where the kids feel relaxed and safe. "From the evidence I've seen, babies need someone to care for them who loves them, but it doesn't necessarily need to be a parent. It could be a child care worker, or another relative."

Did You Know?

Children whose mothers have recent or long-term employment are actually in better health than those mothers who are unemployed for more than two years—just one positive result of the employment of mothers (*Scientific American*, March 2007).

If you feel nervous about enrolling your child in a day care because you feel like he will never get your attention, simply create a strategy for spending time with him. Allow him to be a part of your morning routine, placing him into a Moses basket nearby while you shower and get dressed, or bringing him into the kitchen while you cook dinner.

Better yet, schedule thirty-minute blocks of quality time with him, in the morning and in the evening, around your routine. Spend quiet time with him in the morning, nursing or feeding him a bottle. Spend thirty minutes with him after dinner, playing with his toys, and reading books. Later, watch a Baby Einstein video, cuddle after bathtime, or spend a half-hour nursing before bedtime. You'll treasure the time with him more, and he will feel more connected with mommy.

The Most Common Options for Child Care

There are many, many different options for child care today. They vary widely from state to state, and even from town to town. In general, more densely populated areas have more options for child care. Here are the main categories to consider:

Friends and Relatives

If you have friends or relatives living close by, and they are interested in caring for children during the day, consider asking them if they would be willing to watch your baby. Do you have girlfriends who are moms—or parents, grandparents, cousins, in-laws, aunts, or uncles—living nearby that would be willing to watch the baby (at your house or theirs)? If so, then it could be an ideal arrangement for everyone.

"My husband and I are lucky enough to have my grandma watch our little one, and she lives very close to the office," says Jen, twenty-six, a human resources professional and mother of Isabel, who's almost two. (Jen is also now pregnant with her second child.) "My husband works earlier than me, so I drop her off in the morning, and he picks her up."

Remember that if a friend or relative is providing substantial child care, you still need to pay her—unless she genuinely wants to do it for free (or as an exchange of some kind). Don't assume you will get it all for free. That is not only unfair to your friend or relative, but it may also lead to bad feelings.

Ask your friend or relative up front exactly how much he or she wants to get paid. In fact, you may want to ask all of the questions from your list of preferences (see below). In the end, you may find it simpler to work with a licensed day care provider.

Also, don't rule out using male relatives or friends that you trust. In our case, my retired father-in-law made a perfect babysitter one day per week. Use the same standards as you would with a female care provider when evaluating whether your male friend or relative would make a good child care provider.

Vonna and her husband are both nurses with varying schedules. She says that their decision to expand their family was based in part on their child care situation. "Brian's parents are retired, and Brian's mom loves kids," she says. "They immediately offered to watch our children, and it has worked out very well for us. Realistically, we couldn't have three children if we didn't have their support."

Of course, if your close relatives and friends aren't reliable, then don't consider them as an option. If your sister-in-law is willing to babysit your newborn daughter five days a week but is always running forty-five minutes late, it will only drive you crazy—and hurt your relationship. Find a different child care provider instead.

In-Home Day Care

If you are lucky, your neighborhood permits in-home day care and there is a wonderful woman taking children into her home on a daily basis. In-home day care is exactly that: a person who is running an informal day care from inside of her house.

Dr. Teri says that after trying several larger day care centers for her son, Justin, she fell in love with an in-home day care she discovered. "The woman we found for Justin spent all her time on the floor, interacting with him," she says. "If it was Valentine's Day, they'd be doing little activities for Valentine's Day. He was very attached to her."

This is a wonderful option for many working moms who are looking for a solution that is close to their house, and that feels more homey than a larger day care center. However, keep in mind that the professional credentials (and state auditing processes) of in-home day care vary widely. You may find in-home day cares that are very casual, with no certification, no guidelines, and no formal policies—just a mom keeping a couple of kids at her house during the day. You may find in-home day cares that are run by a state-certified, college-educated child care specialist. The daily routines and policies of these day cares may also vary widely, depending on the whim of the mother in charge.

Despite these challenges, our ob-gyn expert Lindsey O'Neil-Hill, CNM, says it's worth it when you find a great provider. "Jacob goes to an in-home day care center, and I love the woman who runs it," she says. "I really have to focus at work, so this has been a complete godsend. She is wonderful."

Investigate your potential in-home day care closely. Ask questions about the daily procedures. And get referrals from other moms if possible. Of course, if you know the mom, and she is close to your house, it may be the ideal arrangement.

Professional Day Care

When most moms think of day care, they think of the traditional, professional organization. This is a large, open-space facility that has licensed childhood specialists on staff, and takes anywhere from five to thirty children at a time, of all ages. These day care organizations offer structured playtime, snack time, and even nap time—and a varying level of educational activities.

Lori raves about the advantages of using day care for her two children, Addie and John. She cites the consistency and convenience, as well as the opportunity for the kids to ultimately socialize with peers. She visited several day care facilities before landing on her favorite.

Keep in mind that not all professional day care facilities accept infants. Many will only accept children ages two or older. And programs vary widely from facility to facility. The more expensive ones offer perks as fancy as music and foreign-language instruction for older children.

Pay special attention to the ratio of children per staff member. The lower the ratio, the better quality of care. Ask what their child-to-staff ratio is. For example, a day care with a ratio of five children to one staffer (or 5:1) is going to offer your baby twice as much attention as a day care with a ratio of 10:1.

Also, make sure you tour the facility and clearly understand their policies for drop off and pick up, or for accepting sick children, as well as their vacation schedule. Most day cares will not accept sick children, which means another workday off for you (and believe me, your child *will* get sick at least once in the first year). Some day cares also take one or two weeks' vacation during the year, but still require a weekly payment.

Lori recommends that once you choose your day care, you should continually re-evaluate it, to make sure it continues to be appropriate for your child. "Make friends with the other parents who are using your day care—they are a wealth of information. Compare notes on how it's going, on what you see—and don't see."

Workplace Day Care

Does your workplace offer a day care? If so, then by all means, take advantage of it. While very few companies offer this expensive perk, it's a dream come true for moms who are working. You get on-site child care, with no extra trips before and after work—and can even check in on your baby if necessary.

Sonya says that while she was working at Citibank, they opened a day care for employees. "Citibank had a wonderful, on-site day care center, which was subsidized." You will likely still get charged for the actual day care (very few companies offer a paid child care option), but you may get a discount, or subsidy. However, no matter what they charge, an on-site workplace day care may be well worth the saved time, gas money, and hassle of driving your baby to and from a professional day care elsewhere.

Check with your manager or Human Resources department to learn more.

Nannies

While the word nanny may bring to mind wealthy families living on Fifth Avenue in New York City, don't be fooled. Nannies are much more common—and down-to-earth—than they were during the Mary Poppins days.

There are two types of nannies to consider: daytime nannies, and live-in nannies. Live-in nannies actually live with the family (yes, they still exist) and are a great option for moms and dads that do a lot of traveling with their business or who need substantial help managing the household, as many of them do chores as part of their work. Daytime nannies are more like dedicated babysitters who come during the daytime only, to watch the child for a specified amount of time.

The difference between a nanny and a babysitter is that most nannies are doing this as a career. Many nannies are grandmothers, former preschool teachers, or women with small children themselves. Some work for two or three different families at once.

While nannies tend to be more expensive than a professional day care facility, they usually offer the added benefit of helping around the house—such as with laundry, dishes, and light housekeeping. Some of them also do baths, and can drive the baby to and from play dates or doctor's appointments if necessary. They also are more likely to continue to come to work, even if the baby is sick.

I was surprised to learn that a nanny in our area only cost a few dollars more a week than the local day care—and she did much more. Our nanny gives Zack daily baths, outings to the neighborhood park, and lots of one-on-one attention. She is flexible to meet our work schedule and drives herself to and from our house. I have enjoyed having a nanny and would recommend it as an option for anyone who needs full-time (or even part-time) day care and can afford it.

WHERE TO FIND A NANNY

- *www.nannies4hire.com*
- *www.gonannies.com*
- *www.nannyclassifieds.com*
- *www.enannysource.com*
- A local agency
- The Yellow Pages

Au Pair

The au pair program in the United States is very specific. An au pair is a student who is permitted to live and work for a family, while completing at least six semester credit hours of schoolwork. She (au pairs are most commonly female) is offered food and board, and is allowed to do up to forty-five hours per week of child care and housework, in exchange for a small weekly allowance.

The Au Pair Program is currently managed by the U.S. Department of State, and requires families to work with one of twelve approved agencies. Au pairs are limited in the amount of time they can spend with a family; however, they offer a unique multicultural experience for your baby. If you don't mind working through the extensive requirements and application process, this might be the right option for you.

- *www.iapa.org*
- *www.newaupair.com*
- *www.aupairinamerica.com*
- *www.aupaircare.com*

Religious Center Day Care

Many churches, temples, mosques, and other religious centers now offer outstanding day care facilities. What many moms don't realize is that for most of these facilities, you don't have to be a member of their congregation. (In some cases, you don't even have to follow the same religion.)

Religious center day cares are some of the best-kept secrets in day care. They are frequently well organized and well managed. In fact, for many areas, they have now become the neighborhood day care.

If you are interested in this option, find out if there is one close by in your neighborhood. Ask other mommy neighbors if they've used one. You'll learn quickly which ones are the best.

Hospital Day Care

Hospital day care facilities are growing in popularity. They operate just like a typical professional day care facility, only they are located at the hospital. For mothers who worry about what might happen while they are away, this is the perfect choice—constant medical attention available *in the same building!*

The quality of hospital day cares varies widely, just like any day care. Call a few of your area hospitals and find out whether they have a child care program—and if so, what they offer as part of that program. The larger the hospital, the more likely they are to offer a day care program. One of my friends uses a hospital day care through the St. Luke's program, and has raved

to me about the high quality of the childhood education specialists they use, as well as the flexibility of their scheduling.

State-Sponsored Day Care

If funds are tight or you have a lower annual household
income, then you may qualify for a state-sponsored day care program. Don't be concerned that you'll have to settle for lower-
quality care for your child. In fact, many of the state-sponsored
day care programs use existing day care facilities, and even in-
home day cares—the program simply assists with the payment.

Christine used the state-sponsored day care program in her
home state of Connecticut to help her pay for child care for her
second daughter, Viviana. "My friend ran an in-home day care,
so I took Viviana there—and the state paid her to do it. I loved
it, because I trusted her wholeheartedly."

If you use a state-sponsored day care, the program will typically pay for a portion of your day care expense, depending on
your annual income. Some women pay $10 per week, while
others may pay $75 per week. You will likely be given a list of
approved day care centers in your area.

Be sure to understand what you need to do to enroll your
children in the program. Each state has its own unique requirements and its own payment plan. Christine cites the wait time
for processing. "They had a one-month waiting period, which
was tough because I had to pay the full cost of the day care
during that time." For that reason, she recommends filling out
the paperwork as soon as possible, paying close attention to
deadlines.

But overall, Christine's subsidy program was straightforward,
although she does note that she sometimes struggled with the
fine print.

State programs vary widely, and all have different income-
level requirements. Check your state program's website for

details. Visit *www.nccic.acf.hhs.gov/statedata/dirs/statehp.html* for a list of state programs.

The Stress-Free Child Care Search

Wondering how on earth you are going to find the right child care for you? The good news is that today, there are so many options for child care, that there is one that fits every style of job, budget, and personality.

Before you despair over how much it will cost, research at least two or three options that you think might work for you. Try this step-by-step strategy:

Ask Your Friends, Neighbors, and Coworkers for Suggestions

Before you start calling child care providers, spend a few days asking questions. Ask your friends, neighbors, and coworkers with children what they've used and who they've worked with in the past. What have they heard is good in your area? What doesn't work?

Child care varies tremendously from state to state, and even from town to town. What works great in Decatur, Illinois, may not even be an option in Peoria. And neither of them have the range of options that's available in Chicago. You will not only learn great information about the options in your area, you will also start to develop ideas about your own preferences.

If you are lucky, you may even get a recommendation, or a valuable contact. In my case, I e-mailed everyone I knew on a personal level—including all of my friends in the Kansas City area, and all of the women from my women's book clubs. I called all of my mommy neighbors, and asked them for a recommendation. And that's exactly how I stumbled upon my first nanny, Sarah, who turned out to be wonderful.

Decide Which Style of Child Care Is Right for You

Read through the options included in this chapter. Talk to your friends. Think about where you'd like your new baby to be once you are at work.

At this point, you should be starting to get an idea of what you can afford for your area. Some areas are more expensive, and some are less expensive. In general, child care in metropolitan and suburban areas will be more expensive than in rural areas, but not always. They also, in general, offer more options for a working mom.

If you know you'd really like your child to spend time in a religious environment, then narrow your search to day cares affiliated with a religious center. If you want the child to go to an in-home day care, then focus on that. Or maybe you've decided to try to find a reasonable babysitter or nanny for your baby. If that's the case, spend more time in your search looking for those.

Make a List of What You Want

If you know what your budget will be, and how far you're willing to drive to get child care, then jot down your top three (or five, or ten) most important things onto a wish list of what you want. You will probably want to include style of provider, general distance from home (or work), a budget, a preference for infants, and anything else that is important to you.

Don't worry about getting everything on your list—you probably won't. But if you can get at least 70 or 80 percent of the items on your list, then you know you have the right provider.

For example, if you already know you want to use an in-home day care in your neighborhood, but have no idea of where to start, then your list might look like this:

1. In-home day care
2. Within 2 miles of my house
3. Less than $200/week
4. Certified in CPR and first aid
5. A warm, loving person
6. Less than five other children at a time
7. Willing to take infants
8. Willing to keep a sick child

The more specific your list, the better your chances of finding what you want. Once you've identified your preferences, you can turn that list into a bunch of questions to ask your potential child care provider during the interview.

When you are finished with your list, review it with your partner. What things are important to him? If he has some strong preferences, then add those as new items to your list—especially if he is going to be heavily involved in baby duty.

In my case, we decided that we wanted a daytime nanny. When we discussed our preferences, my husband clearly preferred a nonsmoker who would not bring any additional children into our home (several of the nannies we talked to mentioned that they would bring their own toddlers as part of the deal). While neither of those items bothered me very much, I felt it was important to accommodate his preferences—and bring his participation into the deal.

Do a Search for Local Providers

Once you know the style of provider you want and how far you are willing to drive, then you are ready to begin looking at local providers who offer that service. Your goal here is to find at least three providers that you can interview. Depending on your time, you may want to interview more—I've had friends who visited ten day care facilities to find the right one—but at a minimum, you'll want at least three to choose from. That will give you a good sampling of the differences in policies, styles, and behaviors.

There are lots of ways you can find child care providers. Once again, calling your friends, neighbors, and coworkers can be a great resource—even the non-mommies may know of something in their neighborhood.

Where is the best place to find a good list of child care providers? Start here:

FINDING A LIST OF CHILD CARE PROVIDERS
- Your pediatrician
- The Yellow Pages
- Chamber of Commerce
- Ads in local newspapers or magazines
- *www.childcareaware.org*
- *www.nannies4hire.com*
- Referrals from friends

In my case, I was completely naive about how challenging the child care search could be. I was lucky to find my daytime nanny, Sarah, through the recommendation of a neighbor, who had used her as a nanny in the past.

However, when my nanny decided to go back to college, it was time to find a nanny again. This time, I had great luck using an Internet-based nanny search service—which actually saved me a lot of time and money (despite the initial registration fee).

Interview Your Favorite Providers
Once you have found a few providers, it's time to do an interview. Choose your favorite three to five providers, and request to spend a half-hour with each of them. Tour their facilities or invite them to your house. Meet them in person. Get to know the people who may be spending almost as much time

with your baby as you will. The goal is to feel as comfortable with them as possible.

"We probably looked at six different people and places before we found the perfect woman to watch Justin," Dr. Teri says about the fantastic in-home day care they eventually settled on for her son. To help facilitate your interview, pull out your wish list, and turn each item into a question. For example, if you wanted someone certified in CPR and first aid, your question will be a simple.

If the answer is "yes," then move on to the next question. Jot down notes to your answers in a notepad, and mark the provider and the date on top of the page—so you'll remember to whom you spoke, and on what day.

If it's easier, consider taking a vacation day to get all of the interviews and tours done. Or, if available, try scheduling them for morning or evening, before or after work.

However, if it's a day care facility, or an in-home child care, it would be ideal to see the child care specialist in action. If you are interviewing nannies or babysitters to help you in your own home, then allow at least twenty minutes for her to interact with the child, and tour your own home, to see the setup. Remember, you want this to be a good fit for the child care provider, too—not just for you!

Finally, consider interviewing and touring along with your husband if possible. He may have important input about what will (or won't) work, as well as preferences of his own.

Make the Best Choice Possible

Will you find a "perfect" child care? Maybe not. But you can find one that you love and that works well for you—and your baby.

Lindsey also placed her son, Jacob, in an in-home day care. She says, "If I had one piece of advice for women when choosing a child care provider, it's important to have that *feeling* that it's a good fit."

So how do you choose that *one*? After interviewing every-one, think about it for a few days. Talk over what you found with a friend. Review your list and any notes you took. And most importantly, discuss the options with your husband. Even if he's not working with the day care every day, he's still a critical part of this decision.

After a day or two, come back to your list; cross off the ones you feel had a red flag or did not meet enough of your criteria. Maybe you visited a facility that was disorganized and dirty—and you hated it. Or maybe you felt the provider was too expensive or just didn't have enough experience. Whatever the reason, you will probably have at least one or two that you'd rather not consider. And that's fine.

Now look at your remaining child care providers. For each one, figure out how many criteria they successfully met on your list. Did they meet four out of five? How about six out of eleven? Write down the number of successfully met criteria next to each name.

Next, rank the providers in order of highest number of criteria to lowest number. So, the facility that met ten out of your eleven criteria should rank number one, while the place that met nine out of your eleven criteria should rank number two . . . and so on. Here's what my list looked like, after I ranked them during our search for a new daytime nanny:

1. Becky: 6 out of 7 (everything but price—a little outside of my budget)
2. Tiffany: 5.5 out of 7 (first aid certified, but not CPR)
3. Elizabeth: 5 out of 7 (still a good choice, but too far away, a little pricey)

Remember, you are *not* going to get every single item on your wish list. You will probably have to compromise some-where. Maybe you absolutely loved the older woman who cares for two grandchildren at her house, is certified in CPR, and bakes fresh chocolate chip cookies every day at 3:00—but she is twelve miles from your house instead of two. Even though it means more driving time than you had originally planned, it may be worth the compromise, depending on your priorities.

Keep Your Options Open

Sonya, who was handling child care the second time around for her second daughter, Kramer, took a more competitive approach. Since good day care was scarce in her area, she found several day care centers that met her criteria and got added to the wait lists on *all* of them, then she visited those that opened up first. She recommends this for any new moms trying to get their children into a good center in a competitive area.

Once you know which day care you want, call them *immediately*. Don't delay. You don't want them to give your spot away to someone else or get snapped up by another family. Good child care providers go fast!

Decide on a Schedule

Once you have officially hired your child care provider, decide on a schedule. Find out if they have a wait list. Make a deposit if necessary.

Tell them clearly when you would ideally like them to begin caring for your infant and what the schedule will be. How many days, weeks, or months are you planning to take off? How many days a week (and at what times) would you like for the provider to care for your baby? If it is a center, what are the hours they are available? The clearer you are with your expectations up front, the more effective your provider can be.

If possible, start working with the child care provider one or two days *before* you plan to return to work. It will help you get into the routine you'll need to follow, and iron out any problems. Also, you will have an extra day to get things ready for work.

What If Your Child Care Doesn't Work Out?

Whichever child care provider you choose, you will probably end up changing it before your child goes to kindergarten. This is normal. In fact, very few of the moms I spoke to were still using the same child care provider they started with at birth.

Sonya's daughter McKenna went to five different day care centers before landing at the one that was the best fit. Lori also experimented with several day care centers before finding the Montessori preschool close to her neighborhood that she loves.

In fact, many working moms use a combination of two or more solutions to meet their child care needs. In my case, my nanny was only available four days a week—so we asked my father-in-law, our only relative within 500 miles, to help out one day a week. He did, and it ended up working out great.

Keep in mind that if you aren't happy with your child care provider, it's better to move your child than to struggle through with someone you don't like. Dr. Teri points out that many day care providers end up having inadequate safety measures or too many kids. "Don't get discouraged about what you find," she says. "You have to keep looking until you find someone who is really great."

PART 2

After the Baby Arrives:
Dealing at Work

PLAN YOUR LEAVE AND RETURN • UNDERSTAND MATERNITY
LEAVE AND FMLA • NEGOTIATE A NEW WORK SCHEDULE • FIND
THE BEST CHILD CARE • DEAL WITH POSTPARTUM DEPRESSION
• CREATE YOUR OWN CAREER PLAN • RETURN TO WORK (AND
FIND CLOTHES THAT FIT!) • TAKE TIME FOR YOUR RELATIONSHIP
• MANAGE BREASTFEEDING AND WORK • SAY GOODBYE TO GUILT
• HANDLE HOUSEHOLD CHORES • PLAN MEALS • DEAL WITH DUAL
WORK SCHEDULES • MANAGE SICK TIME AND DOCTOR APPOINT-
MENTS • CARE FOR YOURSELF • ENJOY YOUR WORK AND BABY!

CHAPTER 7

Missing Your Baby

How will you feel about leaving your baby after you return to work? You won't know until you go back to work. And even then, you may experience a wide range of emotions that change over time.

What Should You Feel?

"I believe that any and all feelings are normal," Dr. Teri says. Every woman reacts differently. "There can be a full range of feelings, from missing the baby terribly, to not even thinking about the baby," says Dr. Teri. "They are *all* okay."

Common emotions for women returning to work after delivering their babies include:

Guilt: You may feel that a good mom should be home with her baby, or that you don't spend enough time with your baby.

Sadness: You may simply miss your baby and wish to spend more time with her.

Happiness: You may feel happy to return to a job (or coworkers) that you enjoy. It may feel good to return to your "old" life.

Relief: You may be relieved to get back to work and away from the housework and the sometimes mundane tasks associated with caring for an infant.

Anxiety: You may feel anxiety at the prospect of being separated from your baby or afraid that something "bad" may happen while you are away.

Overwhelmed: You may feel overwhelmed by all of the tasks you are required to complete, both at home and at the office, or by how much you miss your baby.

Loss: You may feel that you are missing out on major milestones—such as first smile, first rollover, first tooth. Or you may feel that you are losing precious time with your baby.

Jealousy: You may feel jealous that your child care provider gets to experience these milestones before you do.

What Our Moms Are Saying

Feelings diverged wildly among the moms on our panel. Kendra, twenty-nine, was working full-time for a major apparel company when she left to have her son, Maddox. It was really tough at first for her to go back to work—the first two weeks were the worst.

For Kendra, it was difficult leaving someone else to care for Maddox, and her feelings of sadness and loss are something she still grapples with, to this day. "I feel like somebody else is raising him—and they are not doing as good of a job as I could," she says. "Sometimes I feel jealous of women who can stay home with their kids."

Sonya, on the other hand, loves her job, and feels invigorated by it. "I never missed my baby," she says matter-of-factly. "I'm not a stay-at-home mom type. But that doesn't mean I'm a bad mom."

In my case, I felt overwhelming relief to get back to work after my maternity leave was over. I found that returning to the familiar tasks and routines of my job was comforting. I enjoyed coming back to work, to the great surprise of myself—and my employees.

Fun Reminders of Your Baby at Work

Looking for a fun way to remember your baby at work? Try putting a photo of you two together as a screensaver on your desktop, at your workstation, on your clipboard, or anywhere else where you will see it often.

When You're *Really* Unhappy

If you are *really* unhappy at work because you miss your baby a lot, maybe you should rethink your decision. While becoming a stay-at-home mom is one option, you could also try negotiating with your manager for a shorter (or different) work schedule, as discussed in Chapter 3. You could also try finding a new job that allows you to work fewer hours—or days.

Assuming you can stand it, try waiting two to four weeks after you return to your job to make your final decision. Most new mothers that I spoke to reported that they missed their babies the most during that first month back at work. Many said that it improved for them after that.

If you are still having difficulty leaving your baby after that first month, then maybe it's time to consider quitting your job. If you decide that you should quit, don't feel badly about it. It happens all the time. Remember, there are no wrong answers.

Could It Be Something Else?

Sometimes, your feelings may not have anything to do with missing your baby. They may involve something else altogether.

For example, if you feel anxious or sad when you drop off your daughter at her child care, maybe it's because you really don't trust your provider and you suspect something could be wrong. Or maybe you feel sad and overwhelmed because you are really unhappy with your job, which intensifies your feelings about your baby.

When a mom feels particularly guilty about her work or misses her baby a great deal, then Dr. Teri tries to find out what it is she *really* wants to do.

There are several things you can do to uncover your true feelings if you think that something else may be at play here. Try writing about it for one page on a blank sheet of paper and see what comes up. Talk to a good friend about it. Or simply sleep on it. Try to figure out what is bothering you. What are you thinking when you drop off your daughter in the morning? How are you feeling, specifically?

"Figure out what it is you want to do and how important it is for you to be at work," Dr. Teri says. "Ask yourself, 'How do I feel about this right now? What do I really want to do?'"

When to Be Concerned

If you are missing your baby excessively, are weeping uncontrollably, or are having difficulty concentrating at work, then you may be experiencing postpartum depression. Between 12 and 16 percent of women experience real postpartum depression (up to nine weeks after delivery—and for some, as late as six months after delivery). Symptoms include:

- Fatigue
- Irritability
- Crying easily

- Mood swings
- Loss of interest in normally pleasurable activities
- Loss of interest in the baby
- Feelings of inadequacy
- Suicidal thoughts

If you think this fits your current feelings, you should speak to your health care provider immediately. Don't panic—postpartum depression is not uncommon, and it can be resolved with appropriate care. Almost all the women who experience postpartum depression go on to be healthy, happy working mothers, and there's no reason you can't, too. You *can* overcome the symptoms and go on to enjoy both your baby—and your work.

CHAPTER 8

Catching Up at Work

When you return to work after maternity leave, it's easy to get overwhelmed. You're a new mom, and you're tired. Your job may have changed—albeit in small, subtle ways: Coworkers may have changed desks, or new procedures may have been decided. New policy memos have been handed out since you left. Time has passed.

Of course, things change at work whenever you miss time—whether it's a few days for sick time, or a week for vacation. But normally, the time is so short that you barely notice the changes. However, when you've missed several weeks or months in a row, the changes become more prominent—and may overwhelm you. Here are some tips for what to expect—and how to handle it.

How Will You Feel When You Go Back to Work?

In addition to job changes, throw in a fatiguing mix of sleep loss and baby duty as a new mother, and you have a potent mix for an emotional week back at work. So, how will you feel when you go back?

Don't be surprised if you find yourself struggling a little during the first few weeks. It's a little like learning to juggle—you don't start out right away juggling bowling balls. You have to start with something small and light, like Ping-Pong balls. In other words, it's going to take awhile to get the hang of it.

You may feel like you are handling everything smoothly. Or you may feel panicky, with so many balls juggling in the air that you hardly know what to do with yourself. Or you may simply feel excited and happy to be back at work.

All of these feelings are completely normal, says Dr. Teri, who has counseled more than 1,000 women in her career. She says that none of these feelings indicate that anything is wrong. "The important thing here is that thoughts are just thoughts," Dr. Teri says.

The moms on our panel represent the wide range of emotions women experience upon returning to work. Lori mostly felt distracted. "It was so hard to keep my mind on my work," she says. "I always wanted to call and check on the baby." Later, she came to enjoy her work more as she became more comfortable with her child care provider.

On the other hand, April was excited to get back to work. "Two weeks after I gave birth, I was ready to go back to work. At that time, I had a job with a lot of free time, so I could actually get things done at work—like paying bills. In the end, I took eight weeks off, but I was *very* ready to go back."

No matter how you feel about returning—whether it's excited or anxious—hold off on making any big decisions about work for a while. With so many major adjustments going on (and hormones raging!), you may not make the best choice.

Reconnect with Your Manager

Your first priority when you return to the office is to reconnect with your manager. Drop by her office and let her know you are back. You may even want to schedule a short meeting with her.

You have two goals here:

1. Get caught up on work tasks and what's going on at the company.
2. Show her that you take your job seriously and are ready to get back to work.

Talking to your boss about getting caught up on work tasks is the easy part. Just ask her a few questions:

- What's been happening since I've been gone?
- Is there anything new I should know about?
- What changes have happened since I left?

Your other goal, however, is to show your boss that even though you are a new mommy, you will still be taking your work seriously. Lori says, "I had a great boss, and I assured him he would *not* see my performance drop. I told him, 'I left as a professional, and now I'm returning as a professional.'"

Of course, many managers secretly fear that you'll change from Star Performer into Mommy Mush, goo-gooing over baby pictures and being generally unproductive. Although this isn't openly discussed in the work world, Lynne acknowledges that coworkers often assume that new mothers are not as committed to their jobs. "You'll have to work hard to prove them wrong."

To head off this impression, make a statement to your boss during your reconnection meeting that lets her know you are focused on your work at the office—and not the baby. Even if you are missing your baby a lot *on the inside*, now is not the time for a tearful confession of how sad you were dropping her off at day care this morning.

Instead, when she asks, "How is the baby doing?" speak briefly about your baby, and then refocus the conversation back to work.

Don't Forget to Reconnect with Your Team!

If you work in an environment where you interact closely with your coworkers, then it's worth your while to spend some time reconnecting with them on the first day, too. Walk around the office and say "Hi" to everyone. This lets them know you are back—and ready to work. Make a point to thank the people who backfilled for you while you were gone. They'll appreciate that you cared enough to visit.

And last—but not least—don't forget to say "Thank you." Thank your boss (profusely) for whatever maternity leave you received—even if it was only a brief amount of time. After all, your absence put a stress on other team members. In this case, a little gratitude goes a long way!

Learn How the Job Has Changed

Some jobs stay the same year after year. Other jobs change every day. If you work in a family-run manufacturing business producing steel bolts, your job may have changed very little since you left. But if you work as a waitress in a seafood restaurant, your food specials probably change daily.

In either case, your second priority when you get back to work is to figure out how (and if) your job changed while you were gone. Look for changes in:

- Products
- Personnel
- Procedures
- Location of supplies and equipment

- Customers
- Your work space
- Shifts
- Policies
- Advertising/marketing

Any of these changes may affect your job—and take you by surprise. By minimizing surprises, you can help reduce your anxiety, and feel more comfortable getting back to your previous level of performance.

Get Caught Up

Of course, nothing will make you feel more comfortable than getting caught up on the tasks that have been piling up on you since you left. If you had someone substituting for you while you were gone, then you may not have a mountain of work awaiting you when you return. But for the rest of us, the first few days will be spent simply catching up.

How do you get caught up? Answer e-mails, respond to pending questions from coworkers and customers, and return messages from your voice mail. Double-check your shift schedule. If you did have a backup doing your work while you were out, now is the time to catch up with him or her and find out what's been happening at work.

Your goal is to get all of your administrative tasks caught up so that your body and brain are free to engage fully on your job. If you've been answering questions, calls, and e-mails while you were on maternity leave, this will take less time when you return.

For Jen, who had a unique role in her family business, it was too difficult to find someone within the company to backfill her role. "I'm a workaholic—so I ended up taking my phone and computer to the hospital. I told them I would check my e-mail twice a day. It actually worked out really well, so when I returned, I didn't feel overwhelmed."

Set Reasonable Goals for Yourself

Is it reasonable to expect to come back after a long absence and a major physical trauma and work at 100 percent of your previous performance? Absolutely not. But many women expect to do just that, and get frustrated when they can't.

The best way to reduce your frustration is to reduce your expectations of what you can reasonably accomplish in the first two weeks *by 50 percent of your normal output*. In weeks three and four, you will most likely be at *75 percent of your normal output*. In fact, it will probably be a full month (or longer, depending on your job) before you are back at 100 percent.

Start Mid-Week

Sonya suggests timing your return from maternity leave so that you start in the middle of your normal work week. That way, you'll have an immediate weekend to rest and regroup, which will help speed your transition back to the office and you'll have an easier time getting acclimated.

Approaching your work with this lowered expectation will help ease your transition—and increase your ultimate productivity and enjoyment of the job. For example, if you are a salesperson, and you previously called fifty customers per day, you may only squeak out twenty-five calls per day your first week back. And you may be slower doing it, too!

Why? Because every job—from teacher to tennis pro—requires a certain amount of *stamina*. It could be mental stamina or it could be physical stamina. Stamina is the strength that gets you through the day.

When a tennis pro misses six weeks of work due to an injury, it's easy to see that it will take her several weeks to get back to the top of her game. No one expects her to come back and win tournaments on her first day back on the court. But that's exactly what we expect of ourselves when we return to work after maternity leave and try to perform at the same level as when we left.

Your job requires stamina, too, although you may never have realized it before now. Your body and brain can get out of shape if they don't perform daily on the job. Sometimes, this can actually help us, like when we take a week off for vacation. But longer periods of rest will actually reduce our mental and physical performance.

You probably don't remember, but it took awhile to build up to fifty calls a day. New employees can't just walk in the door and do what you were doing before you left on maternity leave, especially if you were a star performer.

Not only that, but just like the injured tennis pro, your body has also sustained a physical trauma: You've given birth. That puts a serious strain on your body, whether you have a vaginal birth or a C-section. (Never mind the additional complications that can arise!) Add to that a lack of sleep, and you may not be as ready to jump back into the game as you think.

So take it easy. Set reasonable goals for your first week. Shoot for 50 percent of what you normally achieve at work. You'll be glad you did. You'll not only feel more enjoyment of your work, you'll also get up to speed more quickly—without sustaining another injury.

Create a "Plan of Attack" for Your Work

If you are lucky, you may not have any old tasks to get caught up on when you return. You may just need to show up, drop your purse down, and get to work. However, if you are like many of us, then you have many undone work tasks waiting for you when you return.

Once you have reconnected with your team and manager and have caught up on your administrative tasks, it's time to create a plan of attack for the major tasks of your job.

A good way to get back in the groove is to sit down for fifteen minutes and write out a list of all the tasks that you need to do in your job. Even if you know them by heart, this will help you feel organized—and you can include all of the new things described by your teammates and manager. Include everything old that you can remember, plus anything new you learned on your first day back at the job.

Writing down all of your tasks will help give you some control over your workload, so that it doesn't overwhelm you. You can also quickly see your progress throughout the week ahead, as you cross out completed items. That will give you a satisfying sense of personal achievement.

The next step is to prioritize your tasks. Which are the most urgent ones? Usually, tasks that are due today have highest priority. Tasks that are an emergency for a boss, customers, or coworker may also get top priority, especially if people are waiting on you. Note these urgent items with a star, a circle, or an exclamation mark.

If you want to get fancy, you can even make three separate lists on three separate sheets of paper:

- Urgent
- Needs to Get Done
- No Rush

This will help you categorize your new items quickly and easily.

Delete Noncritical Tasks

You know the tasks I'm talking about—the ones you've been putting off forever, like writing an article for the company newsletter or cleaning out your drawer. Now is not the time to tackle extra credit assignments. Put them off until after your first month back. Or better yet, delete them altogether. Politely tell the person who asks you, "I'm sorry, but I just returned from maternity leave and I am busy getting caught up. Can it wait for a few weeks?"

Once you get your list down, there are two different approaches to tackling the tasks in your plan of attack.

Approach #1: Attack High-Priority Items First

Attack urgent items first. Getting one or two of the most urgent tasks done first will help take the pressure off you to perform and will help you to get up to speed.

But remember, for the first two weeks, you are only operating at 50 percent capacity, so set your expectations lower than normal. If you used to handle five urgent situations in a day, then set your bar at two or three. The people around you will most likely realize that you are still getting back into the groove and will give you a break.

Handling Rude Coworkers

If your coworkers ask questions or make rude comments about your slower work pace, try handling it in a lighthearted way. Simply respond, "You're right, I'm a little slow right now. But I should be back at 100 percent within a couple of weeks."

Approach #2: Do Easy Tasks First

A different approach is to start off with the easiest tasks first. Since these require the lowest level of mental and physical energy, you can build confidence while simultaneously building up your work stamina.

Start with one easy task. Then do a few more. Congratulate yourself for your progress as you finish each one and cross it off your list.

As you complete several tasks, your work memory will start to return. In the process, you will also gain speed.

My Back-to-Work Trick

When I returned to the office, I tried Approach #2—easy stuff first. In fact, I set my performance bar *so low*, that I was delighted *every day* about how much work I accomplished.

With managing my business, I normally have twenty to thirty major tasks to complete every day. My task list includes anything from writing a CEO's annual message to attending a sales meeting with a new customer to delivering a presentation. When I came back to work, I felt overwhelmed by the large number of tasks I had to do each day.

Although it sounds silly, I set a simple goal for my first day back at work: to complete *one single task*. It worked! I felt so much confidence after completing that task that I actually did several more.

The next day, I set a goal of two tasks; on the third day, it was three tasks. Each day, I met my goal, enjoyed my achievement, then went on to complete more tasks. This way, I was able to slowly and gradually build my work stamina, and by the end of my first month, I was comfortably back to my regular pace of thirty tasks per day.

Of course, the secret to my success was setting my expectations low. Even though I was able to accomplish much more each day than my goal, the easy benchmark really reduced the amount of stress and performance anxiety that I felt, which gave me a sense of relief.

While not everyone can manage their tasks in that same manner when they return, it's still important to celebrate your accomplishments. Try it for one day, or one week. You may enjoy the psychological benefits so much you'll be doing it throughout your first month, too!

Ask Your Team for Help

Don't be shy about asking your coworkers for help. See if they are willing to help you transition back more smoothly. If you ask them each one-on-one, you may find that they will help you take on less during your first two weeks back, especially if you had complications during your delivery or with your baby. Explain that by helping you out in the first two weeks, you will be more productive faster—and that you'll be glad to help them out the next time they are sick or absent.

The key to success here is doing things gradually. Remember, you won't help anyone at your office if you "injure" yourself by doing too much too soon!

CHAPTER 9

Breastfeeding and Work

Are you considering breastfeeding when you return to work? Many mothers do, and many report that despite the logistical challenges, it is very satisfying. Vonna breastfed each of her three children long after she returned to work. In fact, she continued nursing her kids for as long as six months after they were born. "I like the bonding. To me, it was just easier at night to get up, feed them, and put them back in their cribs."

Other mothers confess that it simply wasn't right for them. Kendra, who works full-time in retail merchandising, tried it for a while with her son, Maddox, but ended up switching to formula. "We have women at work who come back from maternity leave and pump, but it never felt that natural to me," she says.

There is no right or wrong approach. Both ways work fine. To help you make the best decision possible, learn what's involved with breastfeeding on the job.

Why Do It?

While breastfeeding (in general) is not right for every mother, many choose to do it, even after returning to work. Why? Because doctors still recommend breastfeeding as the best source of nutrition for your baby. Not only is it a good source of nutrition, it has been linked to many other health benefits. Lindsey says that there are multiple benefits for the mother as well as the baby.

Benefits to Mom	Benefits to Baby
Helps uterus contract initially	Boosts immune system
Reduces postpartum bleeding	Easier digestion
Decreases costs	Provides superior nutrition to formula
Decreases risk for ovarian cancer	Decreases allergies
Decreases risk for breast cancer	Decreases dental cavities

Aside from the health and well-being of you and your infant, there are actually financial benefits to breastfeeding as well. Formula is not cheap (even the powdered kind). While breastfeeding at work requires an upfront investment, it pays off in the long run.

How Much Money Can You Save by Breastfeeding?

I breastfed Zachary almost exclusively for the first nine months, continuing to do it after I returned to work. When I finally switched him to formula, I was in sticker shock. Since we chose to buy a slightly higher-quality powder formula, we spent $23 per can at a discount retailer. We used a little more than two cans per week, so in the end we spent $46 per week, or roughly

$184 per month. In the nine months that I breastfed my baby, I estimate that I saved over $1,600!

Of course, you don't have to do one or the other. Many moms supplement their breastmilk with formula feedings. Other moms start out with breastmilk, then transition the baby to formula. Your only risk here is a decreasing milk supply if you don't nurse full-time. Talk to your ob-gyn for a better understanding of how your approach will affect your milk supply.

If You Choose Not to Breastfeed

Of course, some moms never breastfeed at all, and that's fine, too. Breastfeeding is not right for everyone.

For some women, it's an easy matter of choice: They simply don't want to nurse. For others, it's a matter of feeling overwhelmed—it can be difficult to manage the new demands of motherhood and returning to work, never mind the added challenge of learning to breastfeed and pump. For others, a physical complication may make it impossible to nurse.

That was exactly the case for our expert Lindsey, who tried unsuccessfully to nurse every day for one month after the birth of her son, Jacob, when she was twenty-eight. "I had decided prior to delivering that I was going to nurse for a year, but my milk never came in. I hadn't anticipated any issues with nursing, and was totally blindsided by it."

Of course, if you are undecided, you can always try breastfeeding first, then switch to formula later. (It's much more difficult to do it the other way around, because once your milk dries up, it will take heroic efforts to get it to return.) Lindsey says that while she recommends breastfeeding to her ob-gyn patients, there is no reason to feel guilty about using formula. She feels that her personal experience is a good testament to this fact, and has made her a better practitioner in this regard.

"At the time, I was just a wreck about it—it was definitely a hurdle for me," she says. "But when I look back on it, I have no guilt about it. Thankfully, we have a healthy alternative, and my child is consequently thriving."

Of course, the challenges of working *and* being a mother make breastfeeding too overwhelming for many new moms to even try. Jen, who was twenty-four when she delivered Isabel, said that she decided to put her baby on formula right away. It ended up being the right decision, especially with her work schedule.

What You Need to Breastfeed and Work

If you decide that breastfeeding is right for you, then there are a few things you'll need. When you nurse at home, you'll have everything at your fingertips. But nursing while working requires a bit more planning.

Here is what you will need:

- A maternity bra with openings in the cups, to make it easier to pump while at work
- Tape and a magic marker to label your milk
- A good-quality breast pump
- Storage bottles or bags for your milk
- A cooler (or fridge) to store and transport your milk to and from work
- A private area with an outlet to pump
- A place to wash out your equipment daily

Lori nursed her son John for eleven months while working full-time for a large computer company. She recommends getting the fastest breast pump you can afford—even if you buy it used. There are even pumps that have variable functions and speeds.

A good, portable cooler will help you transport the milk back and forth. You can also keep your milk in the break room refrigerator until it's time to go home—as long as you live close to the office and don't need to worry about a long commute time. If you store your milk in the fridge, be sure to discreetly cover it up—such as in a lunch bag—to avoid drawing the stares and questions of coworkers. After all, not everyone is as excited about seeing your breastmilk as you are!

What about Used Breast Pumps?

While your doctor probably won't recommend using a used breast pump, it may be the only one you can afford—depending on your budget. If you decide to purchase a used breast pump, be sure to sterilize the pump thoroughly before your first use and buy new replacement detachable parts for it (such as tubes and horns). I did this, and it worked out fine.

Aside from those basic tools, you will, of course, need a private space to pump. "Most larger companies have lactation rooms," says Lynne. "Smaller companies struggle with it a bit more."

For Vonna at the hospital where she is a nurse there is a pumping room on her floor, which makes life easier for working moms.

If your company does not have a lactation room, try pumping in one of these places:

- Empty office
- Supply closet
- Empty conference room
- Bathroom stall (with an outlet)
- Your car

As long as there's an outlet and some privacy, you're good to go.

How It Works

When you are back at work and breast pumping, here's what you will do:

1. On your break, take your pump into a private room, and lock the door.
2. Open your bra and attach one of the suction "horns" and a bottle (or bag).
3. Pump the milk into the bottle or bag, until both breasts are empty.
4. Seal off the bottle or bag, and mark the date on it with a marker.
5. Put the sealed bottles or bags in an ice cooler or refrigerator.
6. Wash out the pieces of your pump so that they are clean and ready to go for next time.
7. Bring your stored milk home and put it in the refrigerator for your child care worker.

Pumping should last ten to twenty minutes, depending on the speed of your pump.

Staying Nourished and Hydrated

Nursing makes you hungry—and thirsty. I brought along snacks, water, or juice every time I pumped. While the pump was operating, I ate a good snack and drank a tall glass of juice or milk. It provided a great break in my workday, and I went back to my desk feeling refreshed—and closer to my baby.

Be aware that neither pumping—nor breastfeeding—is easy at first. It can take awhile to get used to it. "Pumping is really exhausting," says Lindsey. "And it can be boring, too."

Of course, breastfeeding in general can also be painful at first. But it does get easier over time. "I thought I was going to die the first week, my nipples were so crusted and cracked," Lori confesses, sharing a sentiment that is common for many first-time moms. "I went to a lactation consultant for help, and it was the best $80 I ever spent. It turned out that my baby wasn't latching on correctly, and she fixed the problem immediately."

Tips for Traveling Moms

Even when I took short trips for work, I still managed to pump (although trips longer than two to three days were more difficult to manage). I simply packed along my pump, bottles, and a cooler, and then brought it back home again. Depending on the current airline requirements for transporting liquids, you may be able to do the same thing, too. Or if you have the option, do a car trip—it will be a lot easier to pack and carry along your equipment, and to carry back the milk. If worse comes to worst, and you can't carry the milk home, you can always "pump and dump" the milk, so that at a minimum, you maintain your milk supply. If you are going to be traveling via airplane, check out the Transportation Security Authority's website for information about travel requirements for liquids at *www.tsa.gov.*

Negotiating Breastfeeding at Work

One of the most challenging parts of breastfeeding for working mothers is handling it with the people at work. While some bosses are comfortable with their employees pumping at work, others are not. You may also have to deal with curious coworkers—especially if you work with people who haven't interacted with nursing mothers before.

Unfortunately, there is no *legal* obligation for your boss to provide either the space or the time for you to pump your breastmilk, but many do. Check with your human resources department, or look at your company policies. You can also try asking other moms at your office. Find out if their managers helped them find space or gave them extra time to pump.

When you are ready, sit down and talk to your manager. Explain what you want to do, and how many months you plan to do it. Ask for a designated private area to pump. If he seems nervous or uncomfortable about it, then offer to work it into your regular breaks and schedule. Assure him that this will not detract from your work performance in any way; in fact, it may actually reduce missed time at work, as this should keep your baby healthier over the first year.

If your boss still does not feel comfortable with it, don't give up. You can always do it on your lunch break or coffee break. Or you can split up your lunch break into three ten-minute segments, and eat your lunch while you pump. Provided that you have an electrical outlet, you can pump in a bathroom stall, or in your car, where you can stash a cooler filled with ice.

If it doesn't affect your job performance, and you limit your activity to normal breaks, most managers will turn a blind eye—even if they disagree (or feel uncomfortable) with what you are doing.

Handling Curious Coworkers

If you're pumping at work, chances are you will probably get questions from coworkers. Don't take it personally—it is probably more about curiosity than hostility. After all, how often do we see pumping (or breastfeeding, for that matter) in a movie, in the news, or on TV? Almost never! Prep a short one-sentence response in advance of your return to work so you feel more confident. You don't have to give a lot of details (unless you want to). Try, "I'm continuing to nurse my baby for the next three months," or "I'm going to try pumping because my doctor says it's the best thing for my baby."

CHAPTER 10

Sick Time and Doctor Appointments

Are you the kind of person who hardly ever takes a sick day from work? Do you pride yourself on your attendance? Or do you struggle to make it into the office every day?

No matter what your attendance has been in the past, sick time is a reality for new mothers. While you can plan for some of the time off (such as for well-baby visits to the pediatrician), much of it will be a surprise and come when you least expect it.

Educating yourself in advance about those expected—and unexpected—days off will help you prepare for them and minimize the stress to you. Trust me, they happen to everyone—even the most health-conscious, well-organized moms.

What Should You Expect for Sick Time and Doctor Appointments?

During the first year after the baby is born, a lot of important physical milestones are achieved by both you and your baby. You will recover from your delivery, begin losing your baby weight, and possibly start breastfeeding. Your baby will grow, (and grow, and grow), learn to eat solid foods, sit up, and even begin vocalizing. She will probably also have her first illness, and get several important immunizations.

Inevitably, challenges crop up. To cover all of these special circumstances, you will need time for doctor's visits, for both you and baby. Here are the most common (and a few uncommon) situations that you and your baby will face in the first year.

Mommy's Sick Time and Doctor Appointments

Your body experiences a physical trauma when you give birth to a baby. While modern medicine helps a lot, it is still a challenging experience. Whether you deliver vaginally or via C-section, your body takes quite a beating and will need time to heal. That healing starts right away, in the delivery room, and continues as you return to work.

For a vaginal delivery, you can expect to be at the hospital twenty-four to forty-eight hours after delivery; for a C-section, it's closer to seventy-two hours, although most insurances will cover up to ninety-six hours postdelivery.

You already know from your pregnancy that regular doctor visits with your ob-gyn are a part of the delivery process. Now, after your delivery, your ob-gyn will continue to monitor your progress, and healing.

Here is the recommended schedule for postpartum checkups:

- Immediately after delivery (in the hospital)
- One week postpartum (C-section only)
- Six weeks postpartum

In some cases, for example, if you had a traumatic delivery with a severe laceration, or if you have a history of depression (which has a high chance of recurrence), your ob-gyn will likely ask you to return after two to four weeks.

Complications are more common than you might think. If you are planning to return to work immediately after the birth, or if you are anticipating a very short maternity leave (fewer than four weeks), remember that physical complications from birth may hamper your plans. In fact, they may keep you home longer than you had anticipated, especially if you have a C-section.

One of the moms on our panel, Jen, experienced serious complications following her delivery. She had also planned to take a very short maternity leave—only four weeks.

She went in for an emergency surgery six days after her daughter Isabel was born. Her placenta didn't fully deliver, which caused her to lose four pints of blood and necessitated an additional procedure.

Also, three of our moms needed more time to solve breast-feeding challenges, which required time with a lactation specialist.

The point is not to fear complications. Rather, the goal is to be prepared for the unexpected. After all, this is nature we're dealing with, and nature has a stubborn way of not conforming to our plans—even if we *promised* our boss that we'd be back at our desks in only three weeks.

Some of the more common labor and delivery complications that women experience:

- Premature delivery
- Prolonged labor
- Postpartum hemorrhage
- Amniotic fluid embolism
- Pre-eclampsia
- Infection
- Postpartum depression

Baby's Sick Time and Doctor Appointments

Amazingly, your baby will have even *more* health needs than you after delivery. In fact, she will have so many doctor appointments during her first year that she will practically need her own calendar!

"Doctor's visits are more frequent during the first few months of life—especially with breastfed infants, until adequate weight gain is seen," says Dr. Kristen. After the first month, the CDC immunization schedule generally drives the timing of the visits.

Dr. Kristen recommends the following appointment schedule for well visits during baby's first year:

- Immediately after birth
- Two days after discharge
- One month
- Two months
- Four months
- Six months
- Nine months
- Twelve months

What will your doctor be looking for during these visits? Here are several key areas:

- Weight
- Height
- Head circumference
- Immunizations
- Development
- Growth
- Family relations

Even if your baby has no major health issues, she can still have the garden-variety challenges that bedevil parents. This includes things like colic, sleeping difficulties, eating difficulties, allergies, or simply a high-maintenance temperament. Dr. Kristen experienced this firsthand with her second child, Sarah. "My daughter was the perfect baby on maternity leave, but then when I returned to work, she refused to feed from a bottle, which was horrible." To accommodate her daughter's feeding difficulties (and her demanding work schedule), she nursed her at night—and wound up *very* sleep deprived.

Often, a pediatrician will discover a health issue during one of the child's many well-baby visits during the first year. If there is a developmental issue or milestones are not being met, Dr. Kristen says she'll refer a family to a specialist—which may require more time for tests and evaluation.

Of course, just about every baby makes a visit to the doctor for illness in their first year. Some of the most common reasons for doctor's visits in children include:

- Ear infections
- Rashes
- Diarrhea
- Respiratory Syncytial Virus (RSV)
- Thrush
- Hand, foot, and mouth disease
- Simple colds

Many Babies Need Special Care

Babies are born in all sorts of shapes and sizes. Many of them have physical, mental, and emotional challenges that go beyond simple childhood illness. Not all babies are easy—some require more care than others, whether they are simply cranky or suffer from something more serious, such as a genetic disorder. While this may not be the case with your baby, it's important to be aware—and prepared—for the possibility. It's also good to know in advance that you may have to make some tough decisions about work and time off.

Dr. Teri says that many of the new mothers she treats do not realistically anticipate all the unique challenges that a baby presents. "Babies fall into all kinds of categories. There are some who are physically sick, or who don't nurse well. There's a whole range of problems you can encounter with a new baby. New mothers don't necessarily consider that ahead of time."

Dr. Kristen agrees. Among the families she sees as a pediatrician, she says there is a lot that you can't anticipate with a new baby. "I have a premature baby patient right now in the intensive care unit," Dr. Kristen says. "It's heartbreaking. The mother decided to go back to work so she can save her maternity time for when the baby gets home."

Of course, many babies are also born with special needs. You and your baby may deal with the challenges of autism, immune deficiencies, speech disabilities, cerebral palsy, or Down syndrome. The challenge here is not only emotional, but also financial. These children require more time and attention, which leads to more time off work.

The bottom line is: Be realistic. You may need more time off than you think. Know your company policy, and be prepared to negotiate with your boss if necessary. Be prepared to handle any unexpected challenges you—and the baby—may face.

Remember that there are all types of kids in the world—and all types of working mothers. Just because a situation isn't perfect does *not* mean you have to give up your job or career. Most parents who face a challenging situation find a way to make it work—and still enjoy their time with the baby.

Medical Care When You Are Self-Employed

When you work for a big company, it's easy to add a child to your medical benefits plan. But when you are self-employed, it becomes a huge challenge. There aren't that many insurance providers that service self-employed workers, and some will not accept infants—or will only do it at great cost.

In our case, it took nearly three months of wrangling and negotiating with my provider *after* Zack was born to finally get medical insurance coverage for him. During that period, he was rejected several times—once for a paperwork error and once because one of his testicles had swollen 1 millimeter at birth (a condition that had resolved after forty-eight hours). I cried with joy on the day that we finally got him covered, but not before paying in full for several doctor visits and immunizations.

Of course, finding someone to cover your infant is only half the battle. Then you actually have to *pay* for the coverage, too! Be aware that many insurance companies charge a premium for infants in their first year.

Do your research. Find out what companies provide medical insurance to self-employed workers in your state—then find out if they will carry an infant. If multiple carriers provide it, then you may be able to do some price shopping.

Be aware that it may take you several weeks to get your baby approved—so start as soon as possible after birth. (You won't be able to start this task before birth, as they will need certain birth records from your hospital or pediatrician in order to provide you with a quote for insurance.)

Insurance providers vary from state to state. To see what's available in your state and compare rates, start here:

- *www.ehealthinsurance.com*
- *www.affordable-health-insurance-plans.com*
- *www.healthinsurance.org*

Now that you know the basics of what you should expect when it comes to doctor appointments for you and your baby, the next step is to determine how you and your partner will handle getting the baby to and from his various medical appointments.

Who Will Do Doctor Duty?

One thing you will need to decide with your partner is who will take the baby to the doctor. While well-baby appointments are easy to plan in advance, illness is a little trickier. This may be a new challenge for women who are used to being in control of their lives. While working moms in general tend to be structured and organized by necessity, you can't plan when your baby's going to be sick. It may be on the day of your important client meeting.

If you and your partner discuss this briefly for ten minutes *before* you return to work after maternity leave, you will be well ahead of other couples—and better able to handle the unexpected situations that are guaranteed to pop up with your baby during the first year. For example, now is the time to figure out if one of you has a fear of doctor's offices, or one of you really wants to be the one to cuddle the baby if she is sick, or that one person's travel schedule makes it impossible to leave work on short notice for an illness.

That initial conversation gets you started and can head off major arguments later. But when the day finally comes that you spend a sleepless night with a crying baby who has a 103-degree fever, you'll still need to make a game-time decision. Who stays home from work? Who takes the baby to the doctor?

It may be different every time the baby is sick. Know that it will most likely depend on the following factors:

- Your available sick days
- Flexibility in your general work schedule
- Your particular schedules that day
- The more lenient manager/company policy
- Any critical work situations occurring that day
- Who wants to go most
- Who went last time

Whoever goes to the doctor, plan to take a minimum of two hours off of work—up to as much as half a day. Your actual time needed will depend on how busy the clinic or doctor's office is and whether or not your baby will need follow-up tests. You will also need adequate time to bring the baby to and from the office and then back to day care, as well as time to get yourself back to work.

What If You Are a Single Mom?

If you can't get the time off, then ask a friend, neighbor, or family member you trust to take the baby to the doctor. It never hurts to ask! Write down a list of symptoms and any medication you've given the baby, and ask them to take it along and show the doctor.

If your baby has a virus or infectious illness, your day care may not accept him back until he is well. This is to prevent the illness from spreading through the kids like wildfire. In that case, plan for one of you to take time off to care for the baby (or alternate days, if the illness runs for several days). If you are in a pinch, you can also try asking a family member or friend to watch your sick baby. If your baby is cared for by family or a nanny, call ahead and check with them first—some don't mind caring for a sick child; some do.

Handling Sick Time with Your Boss

After taking so much time off for maternity leave, you may be hesitant to ask your manager for more time off for sick time and doctor visits. After all, you don't know how they will react. Unfortunately, poor treatment by managers is a fact of life for many new mothers. Sometimes this stems from resentment; sometimes managers simply don't understand, especially if they don't have children themselves.

"I have seen a lot of women who are treated unfairly at work, whose supervisors won't let them change work schedules," says Dr.Teri, who says that many managers (both male and female) resent the time off and "special treatment" new mothers receive.

Kendra encountered one such manager. "I had a boss with no children," Kendra says. "She was a workaholic, staying until 8:00 at night, then coming in on weekends. She expected me to do the same. She had no idea what I was going through."

However, the reality is that sick time and doctor appointments are a part of life for every new mom. So how do you handle it with your manager?

Start by addressing it up front with your boss. By discussing it with her directly, you may defuse resentment that can build up and prevent frustration every time you need a day off for illness or a well-baby visit.

Schedule a time to talk with your manager when she is relaxed. Wait until you've been back on the job for a few weeks—don't hit her up right away. Give her a chance to see that you are serious about your work.

Emphasize your reliability and commitment to the job. Start the conversation by saying, "Now that I am back on the job, I will need a small amount of time off later this year for doctor's appointments for the baby, and probably for illness, too. Do you foresee any issue with that?" By soliciting your manager's opinion, you open the door for her to share any frustrations with you up front.

Show empathy with your boss's concerns. Who knows? Perhaps she was denied time off at some point for sick time. Or maybe she is just afraid she will have to work harder to compensate for your time off. Nod politely and say, "Thank you for sharing that with me," then address the issue she raises.

Finally, make a clear statement that shows your commitment to the job. For example, "This will not affect my work performance or my commitment to my job. I enjoy working here, and I want to do whatever I can to make this easier for you." This shows that you not only care about your job, but you care about your boss, too. You may want to add that the baby's father will also be contributing by handling many of the visits (if applicable).

Next, find out how much sick time you actually have available for the year. You can either ask your manager directly or check with human resources or your company policy. Learn as much as you can about your company's policy (and state law) handling sick time.

Legal expert Lynne says that in some cases, the Family and Medical Leave Act (FMLA) may apply. FMLA applies to taking care of your own serious health condition or the serious health condition of your family. However, Lynne points out that there are many restrictions on FMLA leave. "FMLA does not apply at all if you've been working for an employer for less than a year or if the company has fewer than fifty employees." Also, pay attention to what other parents are getting for time off. "The key is, they can't discriminate," says Lynne. If one mother gets two weeks of additional sick time to care for a sick child, then your company should provide that same time off for other mothers.

In the end, women still occasionally encounter discrimination when they request time off to care for their kids. In fact, there is not yet any federal law requiring all companies to give you time off to take care of your children, and there is a whole new area of the law called "family responsibility discrimination."

Whenever possible, schedule your ob-gyn follow-up appointments and well-baby visits outside normal work hours— either early in the morning, in the afternoon, or on your day off. This may also minimize some tension with your manager, since you are taking the initiative to do this on your own time. Getting your partner's participation on the unexpected illnesses will also help with this.

If you've maxed out your sick time, and your boss is unhappy that you need to take yet another day off, offer to compromise with your manager in some way. Take unpaid time, or come in on the weekend to make up the work. Or find your own substitute at work who is willing to cover for you while you are gone. At a minimum, your initiative will demonstrate how much you care about your boss—and your job.

Lastly, give your manager as much notice as possible when you need to miss time. Let her know about regularly scheduled doctor appointments well in advance. And call immediately if you—or your baby—are sick. You can even leave a voice mail at the office in the middle of the night. Don't cause additional frustration for your manager by waiting until you are already late for work to let her know you won't be coming in—that's sloppy and unprofessional, and it will only make your boss angry (and rightfully so).

PART 3

After the Baby:
Dealing at Home

PLAN YOUR LEAVE AND RETURN • UNDERSTAND MATERNITY
LEAVE AND FMLA • NEGOTIATE A NEW WORK SCHEDULE • FIND
THE BEST CHILD CARE • DEAL WITH POSTPARTUM DEPRESSION
• CREATE YOUR OWN CAREER PLAN • RETURN TO WORK (AND
FIND CLOTHES THAT FIT!) • TAKE TIME FOR YOUR RELATIONSHIP
• MANAGE BREASTFEEDING AND WORK • SAY GOODBYE TO GUILT
• HANDLE HOUSEHOLD CHORES • PLAN MEALS • DEAL WITH DUAL
WORK SCHEDULES • MANAGE SICK TIME AND DOCTOR APPOINT-
MENTS • CARE FOR YOURSELF • ENJOY YOUR WORK AND BABY!

CHAPTER 11
Household Responsibilities

Think chores and preparing meals are no big deal? Once you have a baby, the intensity of housework changes completely. Even if you only live in a small apartment, you will be amazed by how much more you have to do every day. The change in this single everyday task can be overwhelming for many new moms—and can launch a thousand arguments between partners.

House chores change in three important ways after baby arrives:

1. There are *more chores* to do.
2. You have *less time* to do them.
3. You now have to perform your chores and prepare meals *while watching your baby*.

This additional workload can create incredible stress on your relationship with your partner, which can have a devastating effect in a relationship that is already strained by the triple threat of taking care of a demanding infant, working full-time jobs, and learning new roles as parents.

Let me paint a picture for you of house chores before versus after baby. In my life before baby, I probably spent three hours each month doing laundry. This was generally a pleasant affair. Two Sunday evenings a month, I tossed a couple of loads into the washer, then leisurely read *People* magazine and sipped a Diet Coke while I waited for the dryer to finish running. Total time: three hours.

Here is how it works now. I rush downstairs at 6:30 A.M. with Zack chasing behind me (he is now two and a half years old). I have his blankets, Tigger, frog, red bear, and his Thomas the Tank Engine pajamas in one hand, and a fifty-pound basket of laundry in the other hand. I have only forty-five minutes to get him diapered, dressed, and fed (as well as get myself ready for the day) and get one load of laundry washed and one load of laundry dried before work starts. While I'm eating breakfast and keeping Zack out of the knife drawer, I am also trying to get yesterday's laundry folded because my husband has no clean boxer shorts and there is only one clean towel left in the closet. As you can see, things have changed a little!

So what can you do? To prevent house chores from over-whelming you (and your marriage), you'll need to look calmly at the situation, head-on. Here's a strategic breakdown on house chores that will put you ahead of the game. In the second half of the chapter, we'll focus on ways to make meal preparation easier.

What Needs to Get Done?

The challenge here is that when you are rushing to finish chores in a time crunch, it is so much easier to snap at your partner or your child. Of course, that only makes things worse.

Take a step back and assess the situation beforehand, while you feel calm and in control. The first thing you can do is to understand exactly what chores need to get done. What tasks must be done to keep *your* household running, now that the baby is here? And how can you reduce the total time you spend on house chores?

Of course, you will still have all the same chores to do that you did previously. But some of those chores will now need to be done more frequently, and some will involve a lot more time (or effort). Some of those chores will now become less important, and may even drop off your list. And now, with the baby, you will have many totally new chores to do.

Start by gathering some information. Ask yourself:

- How much time are you spending each week on laundry, dishes, mopping, and so on?
- How much time is your partner spending each week on car washes, cooking, shopping, and so on?

This will give you some objectivity and will help focus your energy on solving the challenge of fitting everything in—rather than getting frustrated or yelling at your partner or child.

Make a list of all the chores that each of you do, as well as how much time you spend each week doing them. Don't forget the little stuff that you do every week—like getting gas, buying groceries, washing the car, and going to the post office. You may be surprised at how much you are actually doing in a week.

Once you have your list down, you can begin adding up your totals. Add up how much time each of you is spending on house chores weekly and the total for both of you.

Now ask yourself:

- Is this split fair and reasonable to both of you?
- Are you spending too much (or not enough) time on house chores?
- Is there a way to reduce the total time you are spending on house chores?

Now you have a tool to evaluate who is doing what. You can refer back to the list (and update it as needed). Or, if your work situation changes, then you can redo the list completely.

The goal is to find a way to tackle the house chores that is comfortable for both of you, with all the commitments you each have. This list is a start—it's not the final answer. But you can use it to help you both decide whether one person is shouldering too much of the burden.

Of course, not every couple has difficulty sharing the house chores. Many find creative ways to compromise. Kendra, who had been married for three years before she had her son, says that her husband has always been helpful, long before the baby came.

"Brody has always helped me with housework," she says. "If I'm late, he'll make dinner."

And that's really the key—it's whatever works for you. There's no right (or wrong) answer here. If your list looks fine and you are both satisfied with the arrangement you have, then there's no need to change it. Because at the end of the day, it doesn't really matter who does what—only that you are both happy with it.

But if you are not happy with your current arrangement, then try one of the following strategies for minimizing house chores after baby. They will help you not only get more time with your baby and partner, they will also help you to be happier with your time spent on chores.

Strategies for Minimizing House Chores after Baby

You can help yourself (and your partner) by reducing the house chores as much as possible after baby arrives. Even if you only decide to reduce the house chores for the first six months, or year, after you return to work, it will be worth it. Trust me—no sane woman expects your house to look as good as it did before the baby arrived. Take advantage of the fact that people expect a new mother to have a messy house, and take the stress off yourself by minimizing your total house chore burden. Your relationship with your partner will likely benefit, too. Here are some strategies for minimizing those challenging house chores.

Get Rid of Nonessential Chores

The easiest and best thing you can do for yourself is to get rid of the nonessential tasks on your house chore list.

That probably sounds crazy. You're probably thinking, *But how can I go without cleaning our master bathroom? That's impossible!*

I'm not asking you to put off cleaning forever. Just for the first three months (to a year) after you return to work. You simply have different priorities right now, and it will be pure insanity to try to do all of the house chores you have done in the past in addition to working, watching the baby, keeping your relationship alive—and, well . . . *living.*

Here's how you do it. Take a look at your house chores list. Now, identify a few tasks on the list that are less important. Ask yourself, "What can I live without for *three months?* What would not impact my quality of life if I simply didn't do it?"

Of course, you are probably going to have to do grocery shopping, cooking, laundry, and dishes. Those are the Big Four that you can't get around because those impact you every day. You could not go for too many days without eating or without clean clothes.

But what about the other tasks on your list? How long could you go without washing your car? Or redecorating the bathroom? Or reorganizing the downstairs closet? Probably a pretty long time. Which makes them good candidates for nonessential tasks.

These are exactly the kind of tasks you want to target. Take them off your list. Make it a goal to remove at least five of the nonessential chores from your list. Just go ahead and put a big red line through them—you are excused from doing them for three months (or for up to a year, depending on how busy you are—it's your call). You will reduce the pressure on yourself, and possibly even save your marriage. So don't wait—do it now!

The Bonus of Temporarily Removing Nonessential Chores

I discovered that some of the chores I was doing before were so inessential that they never returned to my list . . . *ever*! I was doing chores that were not really contributing to our lives in any way; I was just doing them because I had the time (things like moving around summer and winter clothes, dusting the "good dishes," reorganizing the storage area, etc.). When they didn't return, I never missed them. You might discover the same bonus.

Reduce the Frequency of Your Chores

Are you vacuuming once a week? If so, would it hurt to vacuum once every other week? Or even once a month?

The reality is that you probably don't need to do some of your house chores as frequently as you have done in the past. The lawn can be mowed twice a month instead of once a week; cars can be washed annually as far as I'm concerned.

Find a way to reduce the frequency of doing at least five of your house chores. Mark the new frequencies down next to the task on your list. For example, if you've been mopping weekly, cross out "weekly" and write "monthly."

If you are a neat freak, remember that it's not forever. It's only for the first three (to twelve) months after you return to work, to help you get adjusted again. Now is the time to enjoy your baby, not your housework!

Be a Little Less Clean

Once upon a time, did you spend two hours polishing the wood in your living room so that it looked *just right*? Could you see the sunshine gleaming through your crystal-clear windows? Was it difficult to find a speck of dust on your linoleum floor? Back then, the mirror sparkled, the towels were arranged just so, and everything smelled so . . . fresh.

If you are the type of person that enjoys a perfectly clean house, then one of the best things you can do for yourself is to reduce your expectations of how clean your house should be. That's right—here is the one time in your life when it's okay to be a little less clean, so enjoy it.

How much should you reduce your expectations? The decision is up to you, but my advice is to lower them as much as you can tolerate. If you are normally living in an A+ house, try bringing it down to a B. If you normally score a B, try for a C, and see what happens. While the level of cleanliness may irritate you at first, remember that in the long term, you are getting to spend more time with yourself, your baby, and your husband—the three most important things in your life right now. After all, nobody's dying wish is, "I wish I had done more housework!"

Let's look at it this way. Suppose you only have two hours to clean on your weekend. You could spend two hours making one bathroom A+ clean, by polishing the mirrors, sweeping and mopping, scrubbing the toilet, and polishing the sink to a fine polish. You could even take a toothbrush and wash the dirt off those little nubby things on the base of the toilet, plus all the baseboards around the bottom. But in fifteen minutes, you could easily get it B clean, by cleaning up the clutter, wiping down the sink and toilet, replacing the towels and emptying the trash. See the difference?

In other words, in fifteen minutes, you can make any room look presentable and functional. That's your new goal: presentable and functional, rather than pretty or lovely or even shiny.

(You'll have plenty of time to achieve those goals after the kids are grown up.)

Meanwhile, after your fifteen minutes are done in the bathroom, you still have one hour and forty-five minutes left of your cleaning time to clean other areas of the house. In fact, you could spend fifteen minutes each in the kitchen, living room, bedroom, baby's room . . . and still have time left over. By reducing your expectations from A+ to B, or from B to C, you suddenly become more efficient—and can do more in less time. You will also be happier with life in general, since you won't be spending so much time doing house chores.

How to Clean a Room in Fifteen Minutes

Can you really clean a room in fifteen minutes? Sure. It just won't be as clean as it used to be. But as long as you have properly reduced your expectations about just how clean is *clean*, then you can learn to do it—and be happy with the results. All it requires is a different approach.

When I used to clean a room, I started with one thing and worked my way around the room, cleaning everything in it. Now when I tackle a room, I look around and say, "What's the number one thing I can do to make this room cleaner?"

Usually, it's cleaning up clutter—the papers, toys, dirty dishes, and clothes lying around. So I set my timer for fifteen minutes and try to get as much done as I can before the buzzer goes off.

If I finish cleaning the clutter and I still have time left before the buzzer goes off, then I ask myself, "What's the number two thing I can do to make this room cleaner?" And I do it. Very often, it's wiping down the surfaces, like the counters or the sink. But if the counters are already B clean, I'll move on to the next thing.

After I finish my second task, I ask myself, "What's the number three thing I can do to make this room cleaner?" And so on, until my buzzer goes off. (If you have more time—or fewer rooms—then set your timer for twenty or thirty minutes.)

What Will My Guests Think?

If you have friends and family visiting regularly, it's okay to tell them, "I'm so sorry, but between work and the baby this week, I did not have time to clean the house." But if you really want to make it look nice for them, then double your time spent on each room and focus only on the rooms they will be visiting. For example, if your parents really only sit in the living room, then just clean up the living room and the bathroom—and skip the rest. Just shut the doors, or turn off the lights. (And if they still don't like it, then tell them in the future that your house is not clean enough for guests. They'll either stop complaining, or stop visiting for a while!)

Ask for Help

If you are married and find yourself doing most of the house chores—or if you are single, and must do all of the house chores—then maybe it's time to ask for help.

Many women have difficulty asking for help with the house chores. Even some married women assume that they must take most of the responsibility for the house chores; or sometimes they do it out of habit.

Lori was in that boat. She says that looking back on her experience, she doesn't know why she waited so long to ask her husband for help.

"I was the one doing everything for the baby—giving him a bath, changing his diapers, and playing with him," she says, while her husband stood on the sidelines. By the time baby number two came along, Lori realized she needed to make a change. "I felt tired and grouchy and resentful of my husband," she admits.

So when she asked him to help with specific chores, Lori was surprised to find he was ready and willing. She wished she hadn't wasted so much time trying to be Wonder Mom before asking for help.

"He did fine, once I finally let him help," she says. "The problem was, I kept waiting for him to offer to help—but he never did."

If this is your situation, then pull out your task list, look over the house chores you are doing, and identify two or three tasks that you would like his help with. When you are feeling calm (not frustrated!), tell him, "I am struggling to work, take care of the baby, and also do the dishes. Can you help me with the dishes, on Mondays, Tuesdays, and Wednesdays?" By making your request specific, and giving actual times and dates, you have a better chance of success.

Another approach is to show him your task list compared to his. If there is an obvious imbalance, you can say, "I'm doing a lot of the house chores right now and I'm having difficulty balancing everything with work and the baby. I need your help with these chores." And let him choose which chores to help with.

Even if you're a single mom, don't be shy about asking family members or friends for help. Some people really enjoy doing housework—and some people really just enjoy helping other people out. It never hurts to ask! After all, if they say "no," you'll be no worse off than you are right now.

Be specific in your requests to family and friends. Request a specific house chore. Put a time limit on it, if necessary. Say, "I am really struggling to work, take care of the baby, and take care of my apartment. I'm wondering if you would be interested in helping me out with doing my *laundry* for the next *four weeks* while I work the night shift?"

Or, better yet, ask them to come to your house and play with the baby for an hour a week while *you* do the house chores. An extra hour a week may be all you need, and many people will enjoy playing with the baby more than cleaning.

Do a Little Every Day

In the past, you probably spent one weekend day each week (or month) cleaning. With only one (or two) adults to care for, this was easy. However, once the baby arrives, you may not be able to get all of your chores done in one day. Not only that, but you may feel less excited about giving up a whole day to do chores—and that's perfectly okay.

Christine, mother of four, says that the best way she's found to tackle house chores is to do a little every day. "I straighten up every night after the kids go to bed," she says. "At a minimum, I try to keep on top of the laundry, because I hate when that piles up. If I didn't do it regularly, I'd be buried."

Hire Help

Think that housekeepers are only for rich people? Not any more. Believe it or not, I have met mothers from all walks of life who use housekeepers—from single moms, to working-class moms, to urban and rural moms.

Housekeeping is not like it used to be. In fact, it can be infrequent and inexpensive, depending on the service you use.

If you are really struggling with the house chores, do some research. Find out whether you can afford to hire some help for those first three months (or even twelve months) back at work. It will reduce stress, save you time, and minimize fights with dad over who does what.

April says that hiring a housekeeper once a month saved her relationship. "I call the housekeeper our marriage counselor because we fight about chores when we don't have one," she says. Even if you're sure you can't possibly afford it, do a little research anyway. Call three places for price quotes. Then ask if there is any way to get that price down. Here are three ways to reduce the total cost of housekeeping:

• Have them clean fewer areas of the house
• Have them stay for a shorter period of time
• Have them come to your house less frequently

If you are like April and the housecleaning is important to you, then maybe you can find a way to rearrange your budget to accommodate it. "We knew we had to find a way to get one, because the housekeeping just overwhelmed me, so we gave up on cable TV for a few months. That did it." One woman was surprised to learn that she could pay for a monthly housekeeper by cutting out her fast-food lunches only one day per week.

You can also try asking for it for a Christmas gift—for you and the baby. Or swap off with someone who cleans houses for a living. Offer to babysit her kids for a day in exchange for a housecleaning. You could also try hiring someone who is brand new in the business, who might do it in exchange for a good referral from you.

So call a few places in your area. Get an estimate. See what you can afford. Then decide if it's worth it for you.

Meal Planning

It may not seem like a big deal before the baby arrives, but getting meals on the table becomes a major issue in a two-income family. Before you spend $5,000 this year on pizza and McDonald's (and gain ten extra pounds!), give some thought to how you (and your husband) will prepare dinner. It may require a bit more planning than you're used to!

The Real Cost of Take-Out Food

My husband and I have always considered ourselves healthy eaters, so we rarely bought take-out food. This increased a little after Zack was born, but still, we limited it to eating two lunches and two dinners out per week — much less than many of my friends and colleagues, who often ate five to ten meals out each week. Imagine my surprise when we added up our expenses for the first year and discovered that we had spent more than $3,000 on dining out! If you spend only $15 per meal, at four meals per week, you will spend $3,120 — just like we did. In other words, one of us was working at our job *one whole month* just to pay for fast food. Yikes!

Set Reasonable Expectations for Dinnertime

If you are accustomed to cooking leisurely, intricate meals for dinner, then you may be in for a shock. With both of you now working *and* taking care of the baby, dinner gets a little more complicated.

What If You've Never Been a Cook?

Even if you've never enjoyed cooking at home, don't shy away from trying it after the baby is born. The money-saving advantages alone are worth it, especially when you have diapers and onesies to pay for. Also, it gets much more difficult to schlep an infant carrier to a restaurant, where you never know if the screams and cries of your little one will disturb other diners. Start out easy. Try cooking one meal per week. Buy prepackaged or frozen foods, so that you can ease into it. Or take a cooking class at your local community college. As you gain confidence, you can pick up a cookbook designed for beginner cooks and try out a few recipes. Keep a copy of the ones you like, scratch the ones you don't. You'll be cooking like a pro in no time!

My husband, Ryan, and I had always enjoyed cooking before Zack came along. We cooked many things from scratch—including chicken fajitas and cheese fondue. But once my maternity leave ended and I returned to work, we quickly realized that we needed a totally new strategy for tackling dinners. So we reset our expectations, and spent more time planning.

Here is what we came up with.

Spend Thirty Minutes or Less Cooking

What's the real secret to cooking good meals and saving money on fast food? Cooking every meal in under thirty minutes. Dinner preparation needs to be as short and sweet as possible, and we found that thirty minutes was our maximum for dinner preparation.

If you are stuck for ideas, there are lots of great cookbooks out there that focus on preparing tasty meals in under thirty minutes. Check out your local bookstore, or borrow a couple of books from the library.

If you already have some cooking experience, then look at your past recipes. Which ones will work well in the thirty-minute time frame? Which ones could be modified to work well in thirty minutes (for example, by using precut veggies or frozen ingredients)?

Write out a list of your fastest recipes to have ready for the future. When it's crunch time, and you are starving after a long day at work, you'll be glad you did.

Here are a few cookbooks targeted at busy moms to help you get started:

The Working Parents Cookbook, by Jeff and Jodie Morgan
Quick Meals for Healthy Kids and Busy Parents, by Sandra K. Nissenberg
30 Minutes to Mealtime, by JoAnna M. Lund and Barbara Alpert
The Weeknight Survival Cookbook, by Dena Irwin
The Best 30-Minute Recipe, by John Burgoyne, et al.
Busy People's Super Simple 30-Minute Menus, by Dawn Hall
30-Minute Meals, by Rachael Ray

Make the Meal as Simple as Possible

Our next secret for successful cooking at home? Simplify.

Once upon a time, my husband and I used to make real sausage lasagna (yes, we even made the tomato sauce from scratch, using fresh basil) and grilled marinated lamb chops with lemon and thyme. We hosted dinner parties for our friends with complicated and tricky menus. Since then, we've had to scale back the complexity (and the cost!) of our meals.

Today, we regularly eat frozen pizza, hot dogs, and tacos during the course of a week, and we are happy to do it. It saves us so much time that it's a pleasure to whip up a ten-minute meal like hot dogs after a long and busy day.

Now when we really want to cook fancy stuff, we save it for the weekend—but only if one of us feels motivated to do it. This approach has simplified our lives a great deal, and has made mealtimes much more enjoyable.

If you tend to cook complex dinners, then consider trimming down the complexity of your meals once your maternity leave ends and you go back to work.

Even if you get back to cooking more exciting stuff later, you'll be glad you took the pressure off yourself with a few easy meals. The first six to eight weeks back to work will be the toughest.

Who Does the Cooking?
Pop quiz:

Q: Who does the cooking in a two-income family?
A: The person who gets home first!

For most two-income parents, the easiest answer to "Who does the cooking?" will be the person who gets home first. If that works for you, great. But the topic deserves some discussion in advance, and the answer may change as your jobs change over time.

In my house, there's no doubt that my husband is the superior cook. I gladly give him that honor. However, after the baby arrived and he was juggling multiple priorities, he did not necessarily want to be the one who cooked dinner every night. And if you normally do the cooking, you may not want to, either.

After bumbling around with a few different arrangements, and having a few different arguments about who does what ("Who's cooking dinner tonight?" "I thought it was your turn!"), we finally developed a simple system that suited both of us. Since we swapped off baby duty every other night, the person who was not watching Zack would cook dinner. It has worked well, and we still use that system (more or less) today.

Decide who will cook meals before your maternity leave ends—whether that's you, your husband, or both. Write it on the calendar if necessary, or post a schedule on the fridge.

No doubt, you'll probably change it around a few times before you get a rhythm that works for you, or when your job schedules change. But at least you will have an idea to get you started without arguments. While you're at it, you may want to give some thought to who will do groceries and wash dishes— another big argument-generating topic.

The Magic of Freezing Meals

Okay, new mommies. Here's when you know you've reached a new phase in your life ... when you are reading something called "The Magic of Freezing Meals"!

The key to freezing meals is to stockpile at least three to five meals in your freezer for the day when you are so darned busy that you don't even have time to cook a thirty-minute meal—you need a ten-minute meal. It will save you money making emergency runs for take-out food. And believe me, you'll have those days more often than you think!

Even if you don't think freezing is right for you, consider doing it for the first two weeks after the baby is born, as well as your first two weeks back at work. These are the two times that it will be the hardest to get dinner on the table, and a little bit of preparation will go a long way.

Stockpiling for the Big Day

If you feel up to it during your last month of pregnancy, cook up some dinners yourself and freeze them for after the "big day" of your delivery. Trust me, it will make your life much easier. Or if you have willing family members, ask if they'd be interested in helping you cook up some meals to prepare for your delivery or your transition back to work. While Zack was an infant, the grandparents in our family took turns visiting our house, cooking, and freezing meals for us. This was no small feat, considering a few of them traveled more than 1,000 miles to help us. It made such a difference. Also, several friends and neighbors brought over freezable meals, which we gladly accepted. It was such a comfort to eat my mother's chicken cacciatore after returning to work with the baby!

There are two approaches to freezing meals, and I've talked to moms who do both. Read on to find out if one or both of these methods might work for you.

Cook a Whole Bunch of Meals in One Day

Sonya uses this approach to getting home-cooked meals frozen for her family of four. She cooks one day a month and makes meals for the whole month. They are all labeled, portioned, and tucked away neatly in her freezer, waiting to pop out and serve the family like hidden jewels.

In fact, Sonya even uses a service to do this. With this service, she cooks with several other moms in a casual, classroom setting, then takes her share of the meals home and puts them in the freezer. Not only does she walk away with enough meals for the month, the service also saves her time by handling all of the prep and cleanup for her. This works great for Sonya, and she enjoys it. It's the perfect "mom's day out" for busy working women—with the bonus of getting your meals cooked for the month.

Cook Extra, Every Time You Cook

My stepmother, Gerri, who was one of the original working moms, convinced me to try this by cooking a little extra every time we made a good, freezable meal—like stew, pasta sauce, or ham. During the first year after Zack was born, we did this as much as possible, sticking the leftovers into gallon Ziploc bags or freezable food storage containers. I labeled it with the item name and the date and stowed it in the freezer.

We've also gotten into the habit of making bigger meals on the weekends, when we have more time to cook. This is when we will cook pot roast and veggies, chicken enchiladas, soups, lasagna, and anything else that freezes well.

The best part about freezing meals is that it saves you time during the week. And when you are a two-income household, there is nothing more precious than time.

Juggling Two Jobs—and a Family

The scarcest resource for a two-income family is time. How do you get everything done—and still go to work, too?

The good news is that while managing two work schedules is difficult, it's not impossible. With a little foresight, it is feasible to handle dual work schedules and still live joyfully.

The best way to handle this situation is to plan ahead—either by writing it down or just thinking it through. I find that seven days ahead seems to work best. So if your work week starts on Monday, then Sunday will be a good day to start planning ahead for the week's schedule.

Planning ahead not only minimizes the arguments with your partner about who is doing what when, but it also helps you avoid nasty surprises (like both of you forgetting whose turn it was to pick up the baby at day care). It also frees up your brain power to focus on more important things—like your work or spending time with the baby.

Better yet, talking through your schedule with your spouse helps to prevent the burden of all the responsibilities falling to you, allowing you to share them more equitably. After all, if you are both sharing the task of working and earning income, it only makes sense that you are also sharing baby duty and house chores.

What Should You Plan?

When both you and your partner are working, there are a lot of big questions that need to be answered each and every day. The biggest one is: Who is doing what today?

Other important questions that you will have to answer on a daily basis:

- Who is picking up the baby?
- Who is dropping her off?
- Who is cooking dinner?
- Whose turn is it for night feedings?
- Who is doing the dishes tonight?

Answering these questions day after day is not only tedious, but can also cause a lot of bickering among couples. These are the basic building blocks of managing a two-income household, but that doesn't necessarily make it easy. A little bit of planning in advance, starting before your first full week back at work, will make your life simpler—with less arguments.

April works daytime hours, while her husband is a deputy working the night shift, sleeping 9:00 A.M. to 4:00 P.M. She says that differing work schedules create a constant source of stress for her and her husband.

"With my new job, I commute much farther than I did at my old job—thirty-seven miles each way," she says. "I may drive an hour through traffic to get home, but then when I walk in, my husband expects dinner on the table."

I had a similar experience. My husband and I frequently argued over who was watching the baby on what day. This conflict dominated much of the first three months—until we finally implemented a schedule, detailing precisely who had the baby (and who cooked dinner) every day.

Your Top Eight Daily Responsibilities

But what should you plan? The following eight topics seem to come up over and over again in the first two years:

1. Work
2. Child care (drop off and pick up)
3. Baby care at home
4. Supper
5. Dishes
6. Laundry
7. Other household chores
8. Night feedings

Of course, you may have more critical items to add to this basic list. For example, if you have pets at home, then someone will need to take care of them, too.

The point is, you don't have to be the one doing everything every day. Even if you are a single mom, you need to find someone to help you. You don't even have to do the same things week after week. For example, you may alternate who does night feedings or who does laundry (either by day or by week). With a little planning, you can vary the routine—and cover the major responsibilities—in a way that benefits *all three* of you.

Planning Your Seven-Day Work Week

It doesn't matter whether you like to write things down or just think them through in your head. But taking a few minutes at the beginning of each work week will benefit you a great deal.

For me, I found that the best way to handle each week was to sit down on Sunday night and draw up a plan on a piece of paper that I hung up on the refrigerator.

Sonya went one step further. She created a "master plan" for her family that covered nearly everything—and she still uses it to this day. Her plan looks like this:

Sonya's Master Daily Planner

Morning	Afternoon
❖ Personal prayer time OR exercise (6:00)	❖ Pick girls up from school/mom OR arrive home from work (6:00)
❖ Shower and dress (6:15)	❖ Prepare dinner/feed girls
❖ Wake girls, prepare and eat breakfast	❖ Run dishwasher
❖ Dress girls (7:00)	❖ Wipe kitchen counters
❖ Empty dishwasher and wipe kitchen counters (7:15)	❖ Sweep kitchen floor
❖ Drive girls to school OR leave for work (7:30)	❖ Empty backpacks and assist with homework
	❖ Choose outfits for next day (iron if necessary)
	❖ Read books with girls
	❖ Put girls to bed (9:00)
	❖ Assemble the next day's necessities

Sonya's Master Weekly Planner

Sunday	Monday	Tuesday	Wednesday	Thursday	Friday	Saturday
Wash, dry, & put away Kramer's clothes	Wash, dry, & put away reds	Set out trash	Wash, dry, & put away jeans	Wash, dry, & put away whites	Wash, dry, & put away dark	Wash, dry, & put away lights
Shop for groceries, as necessary	Empty trash	Wash, dry, & put away towels	Bathe Kramer		Straighten living & family rooms	Change bed sheets
Prepare for week	Bathe Kramer	Attend karate class (6 P.M. or 8 p.m.)				Straighten bedrooms & bath
						Bathe Kramer
Church		Karate (9 A.M.)	Cheerleading (7 P.M.)	Karate (6 P.M. or 8 P.M.)		Karate (9 A.M.)
Softball practice (5 P.M.)				Brigade cadette (6:30)		

You can do the same thing. Think again about your list of Big Daily Responsibilities—baby, dinner, child care, chores. Now look at the work schedules for you and daddy. Ask yourself, Who is going to do what, when?

Start with one single day: Monday. Mark down:

1. What times will each of you be working on that day?
2. Who will watch the baby in the morning, and at what time?
3. Who will drop the baby off at child care, and at what time?
4. How long the baby will be at child care?
5. Who will pick the baby up, and at what time?
6. Who will cook supper? At what time?
7. Who will wash dishes and clean up?
9. Who will watch the baby in the evening? Until what time?
10. Who will get up at night with the baby?

Are there any special circumstances for either of your jobs on that day? For example, is someone working overtime, or is one of you attending a late meeting? If so, mark it down. Then move on to the next day.

If not all of these categories apply to you, then change or delete the ones that don't. For example, if you have a babysitter come to the house, then you don't have to worry about dropping the baby off at child care. Or if you both work night shift, for example, then you may be eating breakfast together, not dinner.

Go through each day, one at a time, until you have a schedule ready for the week. You may even want to do the weekend, if you are splitting up baby duty or doing other house chores.

When you have thought through all seven days, show your schedule to your partner. Make sure he agrees with it. Give him an opportunity to point out any corrections. Then make changes.

As the week goes on, you can wake up every day feeling confident that you know who will be doing what. You don't have to waste time trying to figure it out Monday morning, when you are both stressed and trying to get to work.

Re-Evaluating Your Schedule

After the baby has arrived and you have worked through your first week, sit down and re-evaluate your schedule. What worked for you? What didn't? Now is the time to make changes, after the week is over and you are both relaxed.

Once you decide on your changes, then create next week's schedule. You may want to re-evaluate again after the second week, and even after the third and fourth week. What worked for you? What didn't?

For example, was it too difficult for you to pick up the baby after work? Maybe daddy can try it next week. Would it be easier if one person cooked dinner, while the other watched the baby—instead of trying to do both things at once? Multitasking skills can be very difficult for new couples to learn.

By the fourth week, you'll have refined your schedule enough to be in a pretty solid routine. You may even decide that you no longer need to plan your schedule by then. For me personally, my work schedule was so variable that I continued writing a weekly schedule and posting it on the refrigerator for the first eighteen months of Zack's life.

While creating a schedule may take you ten or fifteen minutes to do the first time, the results are worth it. It will more than pay off in reduced arguments and conflicts. Besides, after the first two weeks, the planning will get faster and easier; most weeks, it only took me less than five minutes to do.

Even if writing down a work schedule is not your style, a short conversation with your partner once a week will help. Sit down and discuss who will do what, in each of the Big Daily Responsibilities mentioned above. Just the act of talking about it will help you plan—and will prevent the burden of the week falling all to you.

CHAPTER 13

Stresses on Your Relationship

For a long time now, you and your husband (or boyfriend, or partner) have exclusively been a couple. It was just the two of you: a cozy twosome.

Now that twosome is becoming a threesome, and this presents some challenges. Think about it: Even if you took away all the other stressors of becoming a new parent, just adding a third person to live in your house would be a challenge! When you add in new house chores, new roles, sleepless nights, and normal work stresses, it can be downright overwhelming.

In fact, in a landmark 1950s study by E. E. LeMasters, it was demonstrated that 83 percent of new parents experience a "moderate to severe" crisis in their relationship during the transition to parenthood. That's an awfully high level of crisis! This study was later confirmed by several follow-up studies in succeeding decades.

There are many factors that contribute to this strong crisis after baby arrives. There are new responsibilities, financial requirements, changing identities for both you and your husband, and even mismatched sexual desire—along with many others. In fact, in their book *And Baby Makes Three*, Dr. John M. Gottman and his wife, Julie Schwartz Gottman, identified a list of more than 600 stressors that couples must handle after baby arrives!

So, will your relationship change? Yes. Will there be new stressors? Yes. But by being aware of the changes, you can identify and anticipate them—before they overwhelm you.

Here's a list of the top relationship stressors to watch out for after baby arrives.

Stressor #1: Dad Feels Left Out

Sometimes, the cuddly twosome between husband and wife turns into a cuddly twosome between mommy and baby. Dads can feel excluded from all the attention given to you and your baby during this special time.

"The one major thing I've seen with new parents is that the dads feel left out," says Dr. Teri. "This happens especially when they're not the one to take care of the baby, or if the woman is breastfeeding. If the guys are left out, it can develop into conflict."

Dr. Teri says that often men report feeling very excited immediately after the birth, but then later feel like they lose their wife as mother and baby become more closely bonded. "The dads feel like they don't have a crucial role," she says. "The problem is, men don't *say* they feel left out. It comes across as anger—and it could be anger about anything."

The best way to handle this is to get dad involved in the child care. Even if he has very little experience, ask him to help with the night feedings, change the diapers, do the bath. Give him instructions in what to do. Or better yet, let the nurses demonstrate for him, right at the hospital.

Once he masters the basics, start leaving the baby with dad for short periods of time (such as a half-hour or an hour). You can slowly increase the time he watches the baby as he gains confidence. Eventually, you can get a whole day to yourself—while dad gets the benefit of baby bonding time.

You can also put dad in charge of a certain task—such as bath time, play time, or reading time. What does he enjoy doing most with the baby? Make this his job each day, which will give him regular, steady time interacting with the infant. The more dad gets involved, the more important he'll feel—and the less left out.

Another factor contributing to dad's feelings of exclusion may be the amount of attention you are receiving as the new mom. "Moms get a lot of attention at this time," Dr. Teri says. "It's all about mom and the baby, and dads tend to get left out. I mean, do you think of buying gifts for a man whose wife just had a baby? No."

Dr. Teri recommends addressing this openly with your partner, as well as making a commitment to spend time alone together as a couple. This can help calm dad's fears that baby will always be first and that he'll be left out in the cold. Talk about the things you used to do; plan exclusive dates for the two of you—even if it's only one hour per week.

"You need to continue to talk about *your* relationship—normal stuff," she says. "Don't just have conversations about the baby. You can't always be focused on the baby."

Stressor #2: Lots of New Responsibilities

Before baby arrived, the two of you had probably gotten into a pretty good groove. You each had your duties every week—work, chores, dinner, bedtime rituals. Now all of that is complicated by the arrival of one *very* demanding new roommate.

The baby not only brings an entirely new duty to your relationship—baby care—but a whole new level of financial and household responsibility that many couples find restricting. You not only have to pay for lots of new expenses—diapers, formula, clothes, furniture, and doctor visits—but you also have to contend with a major list of new household chores, from changing diapers to excess laundry to baby's bath. This is enough to overwhelm anybody.

For Lori, these new responsibilities felt like a loss of independence. "I was married thirteen years before I had kids. It changed everything for us. The new structure in our life—the routine—was a *big* change for us. We both missed our freedom."

So how do you cope with a gigantic list of new responsibilities? First, break it down into smaller pieces. Tackle one responsibility at a time—and do it as a team.

If medical bills are your number one issue, then schedule fifteen minutes to sit down and discuss them with your husband, after baby has gone to sleep and you are both feeling relaxed. Start with a simple, open-ended question: "What can we do about the hospital bill?"

Discuss the topic for fifteen minutes. Don't switch topics; if you are done, then finish early. Brainstorm ideas. Ask questions. Share your opinions. Listen to each other's ideas. After fifteen minutes, stop.

If you still need more time, then schedule another fifteen minutes the next night . . . and the next night, and the next night, until you feel like you have a good, workable solution. Then pick a new topic (probably your number two issue) the next night, and start over.

Don't Forget Time for Yourself!

With all these new responsibilities, it's easy to forget time for yourself and your favorite alone activities—whether that's shopping, reading, or going to a movie. My weekly alone time helped me cope more effectively with all of my new responsibilities during Zack's first year, so I was better able to handle these changes emotionally.

The time limit and "slow down" approach takes the heat out of potential arguments and is a technique that's worked well for my husband and me for years. By breaking your challenges down into smaller, more manageable chunks, you give yourselves the best opportunity to successfully handle some very large responsibilities—as a team.

Stressor #3: Lack of Sex and Romance

The conventional wisdom about new parents and romance is at least partially true: Having sex is simply not as easy with a baby in the house as it was when you were living together as a twosome.

There are a lot of reasons for this. "The big area I see creating a problem is that the husbands want sex, or want to be intimate and close, but the woman is tired, or just doesn't feel sexual at all," says Dr. Teri.

The first reason for this is a purely physical one. Many women have a healthy fear of having sex after delivery, and are cautious because they fear that the first time may be uncomfortable. "I recommend no intercourse for six weeks," Lindsey says. "After that, introducing intercourse again can be a slow process, especially getting back to where women are enjoying it again."

Another factor is exhaustion. After a long day at work, a long night nursing the baby, and a weekend spent cleaning a messy house, many women are simply not interested in romance—or having sex.

"One of the main reasons moms aren't interested in having sex after the baby arrives is fatigue," says Dr. Teri. "They are tired, so physically they are not turned on. But instead of saying, 'Well, let's just try this and see if I get turned on,' they're more likely to say, 'Forget it, I'm not interested.'"

Dr. Teri warns that this is a pattern that can start after childbirth and can go on for years if couples don't try to solve it.

This puts tremendous stress on a marriage. "I've treated at least twenty couples who stopped having sex entirely after the kids were born. While this may be no big deal for the wives, it is a *huge* problem for the men," she says.

In addition, many women feel self-conscious about their bodies after birth. Lindsey says that dealing with a changing body may create self-esteem issues. "Women experience a rather large weight gain that may not come off immediately. That can impact your psyche."

If you are breastfeeding, you may also feel self-conscious about your engorged, leaking breasts. They may also be sore or tender from nursing, especially in the first month. In my case, I was nursing or pumping exclusively, and by the end of the day I was just so darn tired of someone touching my breasts all the time that I didn't want my husband anywhere near them.

And while many nursing moms don't want their breasts touched, it can be a source of fascination for men, says Dr. Teri. "They may want to talk about it or joke about it, which may— or may not—appeal to the new mom."

This can be a risky time for any relationship. If you don't meet each other's needs, then one or the other may look to have their needs met outside of the relationship.

"It's so important to take care of your marriage after you have a baby," Lindsey says. "Physical intimacy is an important component of a relationship, and tension builds when this is missing."

When patients complain of low libido, Lindsey first looks for a medical reason—such as anemia or hypothyroidism. More commonly, the reason turns out to be that new moms are simply exhausted—and sex is the last thing on their minds. In that case, Lindsey advises her ob-gyn patients to schedule regular time for sex.

We Need Romance, Too!

It's not just about sex. Schedule time with your spouse to do romantic things, too—whatever that means to you. It could be dinner out, a massage, cuddle time, or cooking together. Ask specifically for what you need by saying, "I would like to have sex with you tonight. But first, I would love it if you would take a hot bubble bath with me for half an hour." He will appreciate the instructions, and the promise of fun afterward.

"I joke with patients that now they need to pencil in a night of the week to have intercourse, and it's true," she says. "But it's not a bad thing, and sometimes it's necessary. For my patients who've tried this, it's initially awkward, but then it actually becomes something exciting—something to look forward to."

Dr. Teri agrees. "I don't think it's a horrible thing to have sex with your husband if you don't initially feel like it. Try and see if you can get aroused first. Because if you stop relating to each other as sexual entities, then your roles change."

Stressor #4: Increased Emotions and Conflict

Dealing with all of these other stressors is hard enough. Trouble is, you will also need to cope with them while emotional stress levels are running high—for both of you.

How does this happen? Simple. You are both exhausted from working all day and staying up all night with your baby. You may be anxious about your day care, or about things going on at work. House chores are piling up. And to top it all off, maybe you haven't been getting the intimacy you need. This makes for an explosive mix of emotions—one that can erupt into fights.

Be aware that it's perfectly normal to have an increase in the number of arguments you have with your partner after the baby is born. All couples deal with this after baby arrives. The real challenge is dealing with the situation productively and effectively between the two of you so that the conflict doesn't escalate into a continual, never-ending crisis.

More Information about Dealing with Conflict after Baby

For more ideas, advice, and tips on dealing with conflict after your baby arrives, check out the book *And Baby Makes Three: The Six-Step Plan for Preserving Marital Intimacy and Rekindling Romance after Baby Arrives*, by John Gottman and Julie Schwartz Gottman. You will learn research-based ideas for handling conflicts better, as well as becoming more intimate again with your partner.

So how can you deal with these heightened emotions and increased conflicts? Try these strategies.

Break the Conflict into Chunks

Arguments tend to blow up quickly. You can make a conflict with your partner more manageable by taking down the emotion level and breaking the argument into chunks.

Pick one topic that is painful for you but that you feel needs to be resolved. It may be car repairs, day care, or even sex. Schedule fifteen minutes to discuss the topic when you are alone with your partner and relaxed. Brainstorm some solutions. Ask questions. Set a timer.

When fifteen minutes are up, no matter where you're at, walk away—and reconvene the following night (and the following night, and the following night, and so on), until you have resolved it. Then tackle the next issue. This gives you a structured format within which to solve problems.

Attack It Sideways . . . with Fun

There's another way to attack a problem: by leaving it alone. Instead, have some fun. By sidestepping the problem and focusing on enjoying each other, many problems seem to have a way of resolving themselves.

Schedule one hour this week of adult play time, when the baby is asleep, and you are alone together. During this time, you each get something—thirty minutes for you, and thirty minutes for your husband. (If you need to, make sure you get your thirty minutes first, to be warmed up for your partner!)

Earlier in the day (or week), tell him you are scheduling a special play time. Ask him to prepare for what you want, whether it's a massage, cuddling, reading out loud, or a glass of wine together. Then ask him what he wants to do for thirty minutes.

This is a technique my husband and I have used for over a year with great success, and Dr. Teri approves of the method. The heightened intimacy you gain from your special hour together may take the edge off your conflicts, and help you solve them better.

Get a Little Extra Help

If you are really struggling with your relationship, and your conflicts are escalating with no resolution—or you feel tremendous discontent with your relationship—then maybe it's time to get a little extra help from a counselor. After all, this could be a make-or-break time in your relationship.

Know that even if you go by yourself, you may learn enough tips and techniques to get a firmer grip on your relationship challenges. Check with your insurance to see if they provide a list of approved therapists or counselors. If not, then try one of these online resources:

- *www.nbcc.org*
- *www.therapistlocator.net*
- *www.find-a-therapist.com*
- *http://therapists.psychologytoday.com*

There are even counseling agencies that now offer free counseling to families. So if cash flow is an issue, don't give up—research what's available in your area.

There Will Be Fun, Too!

Of course, not *everything* will be more difficult between the two of you after baby arrives. There will be many beautiful, touching family moments that you'll remember forever. In fact, when I told people that I was writing this book, many older couples (some of them now grandparents)—both women and men—reported that those first few years with the baby were the best years of their lives, despite the challenges that they faced.

When I asked Kendra how her marriage has changed since the arrival of son Maddox, she said happily, "I can't say exactly how—but it's different. We're closer now." While they have had their share of tough issues to work through, she says they really approached it as a team. "He supported me through the breast-feeding challenge, which didn't work out very well," she says. "In fact, he did all the night feedings for the first three months, because I was pumping."

So if you are feeling stressed right now about your relationship, don't despair. This is a perfectly normal part of being a new parent. Remember that every other new parent is also going through the same thing you are. You can get through this, too.

Caring for Yourself

PLAN YOUR LEAVE AND RETURN • UNDERSTAND MATERNITY LEAVE AND FMLA • NEGOTIATE A NEW WORK SCHEDULE • FIND THE BEST CHILD CARE • DEAL WITH POSTPARTUM DEPRESSION • CREATE YOUR OWN CAREER PLAN • RETURN TO WORK (AND FIND CLOTHES THAT FIT!) • TAKE TIME FOR YOUR RELATIONSHIP • MANAGE BREASTFEEDING AND WORK • SAY GOODBYE TO GUILT • HANDLE HOUSEHOLD CHORES • PLAN MEALS • DEAL WITH DUAL WORK SCHEDULES • MANAGE SICK TIME AND DOCTOR APPOINT-MENTS • CARE FOR YOURSELF • ENJOY YOUR WORK AND BABY!

CHAPTER 14

Your Health

The number one enemy for working mothers is fatigue. Across the board, the women that I spoke to—including our experts—described fatigue as one of the most challenging aspects of being a working mother.

"Fatigue is something that really plagues new moms for a majority of the first year," says Lindsey. In fact, she cites fatigue as one of the most common conversations she has with her patients.

What to Expect with Fatigue

The biggest challenge for new moms, of course, is that we don't really know what to expect—and we're caught offguard by the tremendous fatigue we feel. Your fatigue may peak immediately after delivery, and then again after you return to work.

What happens? You may feel tired, lethargic, or sleepy. Or you may feel irritable or have difficulty focusing on your tasks.

Jen says that fatigue was one of her toughest hurdles transitioning to her new role as a mother to daughter Isabel. "The biggest challenge I faced when I went back to work was that I was *really* tired—both from being up in the middle of the night, and from being here at work," she says. "Before we had a child, if I didn't feel well, I could go home and go to bed. Now it's not that way any more."

When Is Fatigue a Serious Problem?

Fatigue becomes a serious problem when it impairs your ability to do your job—either as a mother, or as an employee. It can also be a sign of a more serious condition. If you feel that your fatigue is a threat to your health, or is causing anxiety or depression, then it's time to talk to your ob-gyn.

"If you experience excessive, chronic fatigue, then see your ob-gyn immediately," advises Lindsey. "It could be a medical condition, such as hypothyroidism, anemia, or postpartum depression."

In fact, according to Dr. Teri, fatigue may be the number one contributing factor in postpartum depression. "Many psychiatrists now feel that the major underlying cause of postpartum depression and postpartum anxiety is simply sleep deprivation, because moms have such interrupted sleep," she says.

If your fatigue is associated with any of the following symptoms, and if it lasts longer than two weeks after birth, then call your ob-gyn:

• Irritability
• Crying easily
• Mood swings
• Loss of interest in normally pleasurable activities
• Loss of interest in the baby
• Feelings of inadequacy
• Suicidal thoughts

More Information about Postpartum Depression

There are many great books available today on postpartum depression. Check out:

- *This Isn't What I Expected: Overcoming Postpartum Depression,* by Karen Kleiman and Valerie Raskin
- *Postpartum Depression for Dummies,* by Shoshana S. Bennett and Mary Jo Codey
- *Postpartum Depression Demystified,* by Joyce A. Venis and Suzanne McCloskey
- *The Mother-to-Mother Postpartum Depression Support Book,* by Sandra Poulin

What Causes Fatigue?

So why are you so tired? There are several causes of fatigue for working mothers. They include:

Disrupted Nighttime Sleep: Late-night feedings and diaper changes are the major factor disrupting your nighttime sleep patterns. Waking up to a crying baby night after night results in constant interrupted sleep. "The baby's sleep schedule is a huge part of fatigue," says Lindsey, who says that six to eight hours of sleep is ideal, although not always a realistic expectation for new moms. The good news is that this doesn't last forever. Many babies begin to sleep through the night within the first three months; most do it within the first year. The challenge is getting through those first several months of fatigue.

Baby's Temperament: Some babies have a tougher time learning to sleep through the night than others. "Fatigue often depends a lot on the disposition of the baby," Lindsey says. "Some babies are a little more cranky or a little more demanding. That plays a big role."

Lighter Sleep: Many moms become more alert at night after the baby comes home. They may find themselves listening for signs of distress or difficult breathing. Dr. Teri says that if it's not corrected, this interrupted sleep pattern can last for years, even after the children have grown older.

"Some women try to stay partially awake to listen for a child," she says. "They want to be able to wake up if there's a problem, and they get lighter sleep from that point on."

Playing Dual Roles: For many women, returning to work means they are working two jobs—one as employee, the other as mother. Just returning to the demands of work after a long absence can be exhausting, but now you are throwing the additional role of motherhood into the mix. Splitting your time between both of these roles can contribute to your fatigue.

Physical Recovery from Delivery: Don't forget that your body has just been through a tremendous physical ordeal that involved gaining and losing a large amount of weight in a short period of time—as well as the sheer physical trauma of vaginal delivery. "The pelvic floor muscles go through a lot of stress during a vaginal delivery," Lindsey says. "Any strenuous, high-impact activity can be harmful if you do it too early." Of course, if you had a C-section, then the physical trauma is greater—and the recovery is slower. So take it easy on yourself.

Learning a New Job: Motherhood: Learning any new job is exhausting. For many of us, becoming a mother means learning a brand-new job that we've never done before. For me, a person with almost no experience caring for infants, I started on day one by asking the nurse to demonstrate how to put on a diaper. I did a forty-eight-hour "crash course" in infant care at the hospital, learning everything from sleeping care to breast-feeding to cleaning and swaddling. It was scary—and exciting—at the same time!

Tips for Alleviating Fatigue

If your fatigue is hurting your ability to perform at work or at home, then it's time to make some changes. Here are a few tips from our moms and experts on what worked for them.

Get Dad Involved with Night Feedings

To immediately get more sleep, get your partner to help out at night. This may be the most critical factor in reducing fatigue. Dr. Teri says that the added bonus is that dads get more involved with the babies.

"I recommend getting the partners up in the middle of the night with the baby," she says. "Even if the wife is breastfeeding, he can change the baby's diaper and bring the baby to mom."

If you are using formula, then he can "take over feedings every other night," she says. "That helps a lot."

What If the Baby's Father Is Not Available?

If your partner is not available to help with night feedings, then see if you can find a friend or family member (or even a babysitter) that can help out at least one night per week so that you can get a full night's sleep. Even one full night of sleep a week can really benefit you.

Take Naps Whenever Possible

Take naps whenever you possibly can—which is usually easier when the baby is sleeping. The trouble is, it is tempting to use the baby's nap time to get things done.

Napping is critical for new moms. If you can nap while the baby is napping, that's good. But many new moms make the mistake of trying to get things done while the baby naps, which leads to a constant cycle of exhaustion.

Even if it's only on the weekends, try taking a nap. The difference is amazing. After a long week, I spent my Saturday afternoons napping on the couch while the baby slept, and skipped the housework and dishes. It was well worth it.

Meditate

Even if you've never meditated before and don't know what the heck you are doing, you may still find some immediate benefits in trying it after your baby is born. Meditation doesn't have to be fancy. You can simply sit upright on the floor or on a couch for five or ten minutes, and focus on your breathing.

After I came home from the hospital, my father-in-law (a big meditation fan) handed me a stack of meditation CDs and suggested I experiment with them. While Zack was napping, I'd put in a CD, close my eyes, and listen. Some sounded like waves crashing, others had rain or the quiet noises of a summer night.

This worked incredibly well for me. After thirty to sixty minutes of meditation or rest with the light sound playing in the background, it felt like I had slept for four hours!

My two favorite CDs for meditation after delivering my son were Zygon, "Ultra Meditation II" (*www.zygon.net*) and Kay Gardner, "Amazon" (*www.kaygardner.com*). I used these for a year after the delivery, and enjoyed both of them. But there are many from which to choose. Experiment to find what works for you. Borrow a few from the library, or find your own meditation music online.

I also found that five to ten minutes of sitting meditation helped on busy or stressful afternoons. I sat down on the floor of my office (or escaped to the bathroom stall when at a client site), closed my eyes, breathed deeply, and said in my head, "Breathing in" and "Breathing out." This simple exercise helped me regain my focus, and feel less irritable.

While this is a pretty basic overview, meditation is not difficult. If you are interested in reading more about how to do it, here are a few books you can try:

- Victor Davich, *8 Minute Meditation: Quiet Your Mind. Change Your Life.*
- Diana Lang, *Opening to Meditation: A Gentle, Guided Approach*
- Stephan Bodian, *Meditation for Dummies*

Lower Your Expectations of Yourself

One of the best ways to reduce stress and fatigue is to lower expectations of yourself. But this is also one of the most difficult things. It means giving up the idea that everything must work perfectly or run a certain way.

"I definitely see women who feel like they have to 'do it all'—the job, the baby, the relationship, managing the house," Dr. Teri says. The best thing for new moms to do is to be realistic. You now have twice as many tasks, but still have the same twenty-four hours a day to do them in. This means taking some of the less-important ones off your list.

But which ones? Make a list of everything you are doing, at work and at home. Pick three tasks today that nobody would notice if you didn't do. Next week, pick another three tasks. For example, maybe you really don't have to read the book that your boss loaned you. Or maybe the vacuuming can wait for another week.

Reducing expectations also means knowing that you cannot perform everything equally well. For some things you will just have to get a B instead of an A+, and that's perfectly fine.

"It's so important for moms to have realistic expectations of balancing work, home, and life," says Lindsey, speaking for not only herself, but also her patients. "There are some things you're going to have to be more realistic about now—such as dirty dishes in the sink."

The good news is that your body is designed to cope with the fatigue. For me, fatigue was my biggest fear about becoming a mother. I loved my eight hours of sleep at night and was terrified about the prospect of night feedings. In reality, it was challenging, but not impossible. Sure, there were days I was so tired I cried—but I survived. And my situation improved dramatically after my baby started sleeping through the night at around ten weeks old.

Our moms shared similar experiences. "My kids were sleeping through the night at six and eight weeks old," Lori says. "So fatigue wasn't that bad for me." Lindsey says that women are built to cope with this challenging situation. "Our bodies have this amazing resilience to be able to care for our newborns. When we become mothers, we power through and survive."

Weight Loss

In between midnight feedings and work, it may seem impossible to think about weight loss. But someday, you'll want to fit into those jeans again!

A woman of average weight and normal body mass index (BMI) gains twenty-five to thirty-five pounds during her pregnancy. Most women gain about ten pounds by twenty weeks of pregnancy, then about one pound per week thereafter (heavier women should gain less, while a woman who has a below-average BMI should gain more).

Many women are surprised to walk out of the hospital with almost all of the weight they came in with. In fact, many new moms are shocked to realize that the only clothes they can fit in after the delivery are maternity clothes! That's because women only lose eight to twelve pounds on average during delivery.

Okay, so you won't magically lose the weight during delivery. What next? Time to think about shedding those extra baby pounds.

Losing your baby weight makes you feel good. Not only do you look sexier, but you also feel lighter and have more energy to do all the interesting new things in your life. And when you feel sexier, you'll have more confidence. Won't it feel good to get out of those maternity clothes, and back into some of your favorite outfits again? Of course! Here are some ways to begin tackling the new mommy weight-loss challenge.

Set Reasonable Expectations

So, just when *can* you expect to fit into those jeans again? Be aware—it may take awhile.

The moms I interviewed reported mixed results. The one thing they all agreed on: It did *not* come off immediately. So forget what you read about celebrity moms in the tabloids—your baby weight is not coming off in four weeks (unless you are either very lucky, or have a full-time personal trainer helping you six hours a day!). Kendra says, "It took me about six months to fit into my old jeans again."

The best thing you can do for yourself is to set reasonable goals. Remember that it took almost ten months to gain your weight—it's only natural that it will take an equally long time to lose it again. So don't rush yourself.

A realistic goal is to return to your pre-baby weight within a year. But remember, even that goal may not work for all new mothers. "I didn't lose very much weight after John was born," admits Lori. "I was still pretty chubby."

She says that it was not until after her second child was born that she actually lost any weight. "For some reason, I didn't gain as much with Addie, and then the weight just sort of came off after her." Lori is now back to her former, healthy adult weight.

Your expectations for activity should also be realistic. If you are a runner, don't expect to run a 5K two weeks after you're out of the hospital. Your activity level may also depend on how much physical trauma you experienced during the delivery.

Note that activity levels will be different for women that deliver via C-section, versus vaginally. For C-section patients, Lindsey recommends steering clear of strenuous exercise until after their six-week checkup.

So be patient. Start out slowly. Try lower-impact walking for a couple of weeks. Set shorter durations for your work-outs—start with fifteen minutes instead of your normal forty-five minutes. Listen to your body, and what it's ready for, before diving into a major exercise routine.

Diet and Exercise

As with any time you are trying to lose weight, after you have a baby, the most effective ways to lose weight are through diet and exercise. While it can be challenging with a new baby in the house, it's not impossible. Here are some suggestions to help you work diet and exercise into your already hectic life.

Write Down What You Eat

If you are like me, you may have eaten a little too much (okay, *way* too much) during your pregnancy (or while breast-feeding). In my case, I used breastfeeding as an excuse to eat two or three desserts a night—and I still lost weight. (The problem came when I stopped breastfeeding!)

It's time to eat a little less than you have been. But how do you do that? One simple trick is to write down what you eat and drink for one week, and use that as a gauge of how much you are eating. If you feel motivated, you can even buy a calorie book and add up the caloric values of what you have been eating. You may be surprised at the high calorie content in some of your favorite foods! The next week, eat a little less. It does not have to be a dramatic change. Even consuming seventy-five fewer calories per meal will make a big difference over a couple of weeks—and that's as little as three big bites!

The Magic of Writing Down What You Eat

The genius about writing your food down is that just the simple act of seeing how much you eat helps you to eat less. In my case, my ob-gyn suggested it, and it worked immediately. For me, the process of writing out everything I ate embarrassed me enough to stop eating so much! I bought a tiny $1 notebook that fit into my purse, and I carried it with me wherever I went. It worked like a charm.

Weigh yourself daily or weekly and continue recording what you eat. After several weeks, you'll see your weight come down.

Do a Little Exercise

Of course, you will not be able to exercise immediately after the delivery. But eventually, exercise will help speed your weight loss and get you back into your old jeans more quickly.

"For someone like me who exercises regularly, I recommend that they start light activity—like walking—two weeks after delivery," Lindsey says. "But nothing strenuous or high impact, like running."

Exercise does not have to be anything fancy. You certainly don't need an expensive gym, workout clothes, or equipment. Kendra was able to lose her twenty-five pounds fairly quickly doing nothing more than modest exercise. "I don't like working out," she confesses. "So I just walked the dog and the baby in the stroller." In six months, she was back to her normal weight.

Even if you've never exercised before, don't despair. There's no reason you can't start now. And the best part is, you'll start seeing the benefits very quickly, within only a few weeks.

Start with ten minutes of walking per day. (You can probably do that on your lunch hour.) Yes, only ten minutes makes a difference. Do ten minutes per day for as long as you want. When you feel ready, add another minute or two. See if you can build up to thirty minutes. It's okay if it takes four months, and it's okay if it only takes four weeks. The point is to get regular exercise to boost your metabolism.

Of course, you can try any exercise you want—cycling, swimming, weightlifting, dancing, or yoga—once you feel up to it and your body is healed. Find what works for you and what motivates you. If a group belly dancing class at the local gym excites you, then sign up for that. But walking is the easiest way to ease into exercise for a new mom with a hectic schedule.

And this is the real difficulty for new moms: time. How do you fit exercise into a schedule that's already full? Be creative. If you start out small, you can usually find room in your schedule to slot in exercise. Think about your day, and when it might work best for you—morning, lunchtime, after work, in the evening. Are you close enough to work to walk (or bike) there?

Another option is to try to involve the baby. My exercise of choice was pushing Zack up and down our neighborhood sidewalks in his stroller.

April came up with a creative solution. She bought an elliptical machine and installed it in her dining room, then put up a baby gate to keep Ty safely in the adjacent living room so she could watch the baby and exercise at the same time.

Breastfeeding May Help

Although there are no conclusive studies proving it, many mothers strongly believe that breastfeeding helps you lose your baby weight faster. I am one of those mothers, and I feel it certainly helped me. Lindsey agrees. "One of the benefits to moms of breastfeeding is potential weight loss," she says. "Although research has not confirmed this, we estimate that it may burn up to 500 calories per day."

What If I am Really Struggling?

If you don't seem to be making any progress, ask for some outside help. After all, you are juggling a lot right now—being a wife, a mother, an employee . . . and now a weight loss expert!

Talk to your doctor about your concerns. Ask her for a recommendation. She may also be able to give you feedback on local programs that have worked well for her other patients. She should also be able to tell you whether or not your weight really justifies additional action—or whether you are already in a healthy BMI range.

In my case, after Zack was fourteen months old, I decided to go to Weight Watchers to lose the last eleven pounds that I just couldn't seem to get rid of. It really worked for me. Weight Watchers helped me to reorganize my "normal" eating habits, which had changed during pregnancy and breastfeeding, to accommodate the baby. They even allowed children to attend meetings. In only a few months, I was back to my prepregnancy weight.

Whether you lose weight immediately or not, one of the best things you can do to make yourself look better after the baby comes is to buy yourself an outfit that fits, especially when you return to work. When you look good, you project confidence—and that is particularly important in the world of work, where your attitude will signal to coworkers how serious you are about your job and career.

As the weight comes off over the next few months, your size is going to change several times. In fact, I found that I changed sizes (or body shape) about every three weeks in the first four months.

Each time I changed sizes significantly, or my last pair of clothes stopped fitting correctly, I went out and bought one inexpensive, new work outfit that fit great for my weight *at that time*. Not only did it make me look great because it fit correctly, but I also felt wonderful. Even though I still had some of the baby weight, I felt like a million bucks!

While maternity clothes were cute and fun when you were six months pregnant, trust me—they are no longer cute and fun twelve weeks *after* you've delivered your baby. So even if you haven't lost all of your weight yet, treat yourself to a new outfit. It's worth it. You'll look better, and feel more confident—and that will shine through in your work.

Don't Forget a New Bra!

Nothing makes you look more schlumpy and overweight than a poorly fitting bra. Your bra size will change after you deliver, and again after your milk dries up. You may actually find that your breasts get smaller than they were before your pregnancy. So a few weeks after you are done nursing, take the time to visit your local department store and ask the sales clerk to measure you for a new bra. (Most will do it for free.) When I put on my old bras, they all looked saggy—until the woman doing my fitting informed me that my breasts had changed one whole size! Getting a new bra helped my clothes fit better, and I looked slimmer.

CHAPTER 15

Making Mommy Time

If there is one thing that is absolutely critical to maintaining your sanity as a working mother, it is *finding some time for yourself.* By "yourself," I mean *not* with your partner, *not* with the baby, and *not* doing chores.

You probably think that's impossible. Especially when you think about the daily challenges of managing home, baby, and work—there is so much to do!

Believe me when I say you can and should schedule it in. As a mom, you need to meet the needs of your child first, which can wear you out. Carving out some time for yourself will not only keep you sane, it will help you refuel your tank spiritually and emotionally. "It's really important to make time for yourself after the baby arrives," says Dr. Teri. "You absolutely *have* to meet your own needs or you're not going to have any energy left to take care of the baby—or focus on work."

If you are still pregnant, and have not yet delivered your first baby, then you may not yet realize the shortage of free time you are about to experience—especially in the first twelve

175

months after the baby is born. Dr. Teri says that one of the biggest challenges she sees among new moms is that they do not give enough thought in advance to how much their daily life will change once the baby arrives.

"Most women do not correctly anticipate what reality is going to be like after the birth of the baby," she says. "They just don't think about how difficult it's going to be or what it's like to not get sleep night after night after night."

One of the best ways I found to combat my fatigue and "baby blues" was to budget some time alone for myself every week, doing something I enjoyed. Even as my baby has now reached two years old, I still value my "Mommy Play Date" each week. I come back refreshed, rejuvenated, and ready to tackle my work and household duties. Here's how you can do it, too.

How Much Time Should You Spend?

The short answer to this question is: as much as you can get and still feel comfortable that your baby is being cared for. Ideally, you'd like to get at least two hours of alone time each week. At different phases in my baby's life, I've had as little as ninety minutes and as much as a whole day.

Of course, in reality, it will depend on your individual circumstances. You may be able to get only one hour a week, or you may only be able to do it every other week. Give some thought to this. What would work best for you and your schedule?

The key thing is making it *regular*—finding a block of time, then sticking to it, week after week. Blocking it out on your calendar may help you designate a regular time. That way, during a tough week, you always have something fun and relaxing to look forward to.

There are many different times that might work for you. You can try:

- Lunch hour
- Weekends
- Evenings (especially after baby goes to bed)
- Afternoons (such as before picking up the baby from day care)
- Mornings (before baby wakes up)

Lindsey says she wakes up early—at 4:50 A.M.!—to have some time for herself to exercise, her favorite activity. "For me, the exercise helps balance my mind, body, and spirit. I've been exercising my whole adult life. It's healthy, and it's a good release for me."

Of course, if you can get more than two hours, then by all means, do it. When my baby was still an infant, I worked out a deal with my husband, Ryan, to split Saturdays, so that we could each have a half-day off.

It was heavenly. If I had the morning shift off, I would often sleep in, take a (very long, very hot) shower, pick up a book, and go to Starbuck's, where I would linger for hours over my mocha Frappuccino and my book. On other days, I might walk our city trails, bargain-shop for a new outfit, visit a local garden, or even nap and paint my nails.

By 1:00 P.M., I was back at the house, and ready to "tag out" my husband, who then took his turn with some time off—usually to go golfing or work in the yard. I was refreshed, recharged, and ready to go. Those five hours each week saved my life in that first year.

So be creative. Even if you think there's no possible way to fit it in, look in your schedule for little nooks and crannies of time here and there—and for people willing to help. You just never know where you will find two hours in your schedule for "Mommy Time."

Where Can You Get Help?

There are lots of places to look for help with your Mommy Time. Here are a few suggestions to get you started.

Your Partner

If you are living with your husband or partner, then you may have an easier time doing this. Simply ask him to watch the baby for a couple of hours once a week so that you can have some time to yourself.

If you don't feel comfortable asking for that, then just let him know that you need to run errands or get some things done. After all, you do—you need to take care of yourself, and that's a *very* important thing to get done!

Schedule some time on the weekend, during an evening, or perhaps even after the baby goes to bed. Or change your schedule so that one day a week, he dresses and feeds the baby, and drops her off at day care, so that you can get an extra hour or two to yourself in the morning.

Dads Need Time, Too!

If your husband is heavily involved in caring for the baby, don't make the mistake of being jealous of his "guy time." Make sure he gets some time out each week, too—whether it's for watching sports, playing basketball, tinkering with his car, or having a beer with his friends. He will be happier when he returns, and so will you. Plus, you'll be in a better position to bargain for your **own** personal time!

Your Friends

Of course, you are not limited to asking your partner for help. Ask one of your girlfriends to take the baby for a couple of hours each week. Even your single, non-mommy friends may show an interest—and you'll never know until you ask!

If it's another mommy, offer to trade kids. You could each do two-hour intervals weekly, or swap off every other week.

Don't be afraid to ask a friend because you don't want to impose on her. Just ask in a very polite, casual way, well before you are desperate. Leave her a voice mail or an e-mail message, tell her exactly what you need, and ask if she'd be willing to help. For example:

> "Now that I'm back to work full-time, I'm looking for someone who could help me with the baby for two hours a week so that I can have some time to do some errands. Would you be interested? If not, that's fine . . . just let me know."

If she's not interested, don't take it personally. Just thank her and move on to asking someone else. Believe me, there are plenty of women out there who would enjoy spending a couple of hours a week with a new baby!

Your Family

Do you have any family members living nearby? Grandparents? Aunts? In-laws? If so, ask them to help. Many would delight at getting the chance to spend a little time each week with the new baby. You would be surprised.

I recently spoke to a girlfriend who does not have children, and she confided to me how disappointed she was that her sister-in-law would not give her more opportunities to watch the two children. "I love those kids, and I wish I got to spend more time with them, but I'm afraid she feels like she's imposing by asking me," she said wistfully.

Neighbors or Congregation Members

If you are friendly with your neighbors, or attend local religious services, ask someone if they'd be willing to help. Once again, if you are uncomfortable asking, you can use the same ultracasual approach I suggested earlier: "Now that I am back to work full-time, I'm looking for . . ." If there are other mommies in the area, ask if they'd like to do a "kid swap."

Mommy Survival Tip!

Some churches and neighborhoods sponsor a "Mommy's Day Out" or "Mommy's Helper" program, where they send a sitter to your house—or where you can drop off your child for a few hours to get some things done. Find out if there's one available in your area.

Hire a Babysitter

Call me crazy, but I think your sanity is worth a few bucks. When you are juggling work, baby, and house, and you are at your wit's end, a couple of hours of Mommy Time is worth every penny you might spend on a sitter. You'll be glad you did it.

If you're really not sure it's worth it, then try it for four weeks. See how it works. You may be able to get someone in your own neighborhood for a reasonable rate.

I was so exhausted in the first month after I returned to work, one afternoon (unbeknownst to my husband) I hired a babysitter for a few hours so that I could take a nap, indulge in a hot shower, shave my legs, and read a *People* magazine. Best twenty bucks I ever spent. I came back refreshed and ready for work. (And my husband never found out!)

What Should You Do During Mommy Time?

This is *your* time—so do whatever you enjoy most. You'll probably know exactly what you want to do after you've tried it a few times. What excites you? What sounds fun?

The first rule here is that whatever you do should be fun, exciting, or relaxing for *you*. If it's not, then don't do it. If you're finding yourself exercising when you'd rather be going to a movie, then by all means, go to the movie!

Tend to your needs first. Don't worry a hoot about what you *should* be doing—whether it's for the baby, your husband, your work, or your house. This is the two hours a week you get to leave the dirty dishes, unvacuumed carpet, and everything else. Believe me—the world will not end. The dirty dishes will still be there when you return home, two hours later (unless your spouse takes the initiative).

That leads us to the second rule of mommy time: NO HOUSECLEANING ALLOWED!

And the third rule: NO HOUSECLEANING ALLOWED!

Here are a few ideas to get you started, taken from my experience, as well as our panel moms:

- Reading
- Visiting the salon for a mani/pedi
- Eating out
- Napping
- Getting your hair done
- Walking
- Shopping
- Gardening
- Bird watching
- Showering
- Baking
- Bicycling
- Seeing a movie
- Having coffee

- Reading the newspaper
- Doing nothing

So be creative! Have fun. And switch up the variety as much as you need.

What about Time with Your Girlfriends?

Girlfriends are important, too. If you enjoy time out with your girlfriends more than being alone, then consider putting a weekly or monthly "date" on the calendar with one or more of your favorite gals. Or if you can swing it, try doing it in addition to your Mommy Time. In my case, I scheduled a weekly dinner with my best friend, Lisa, that we still maintain to this day. In return, my husband got time to play in his weekly volleyball league.

CHAPTER 16

The Decision to Change Jobs

Okay, so you're feeling like there's a better job out there for you—but you're not really sure. Maybe you've just woken up today and realized this, or maybe you've been thinking about it for a long time. The question is, what do you do now?

As you might imagine, there are some special considerations when you are changing jobs as a new mother—or as a pregnant woman. To make sure that you don't make a big mistake, here are a few key things to consider before making the leap.

"It's such a personal choice," Sonya says. "Either way, you know that there are things you are giving up."

The 100 Best Companies for Moms

Want to find the best family-friendly companies for mothers to work at? Check out the Working Mother 100 Best Companies at *www.working mother.com*.

Understand *Why* You Want to Change Jobs

Before you leave *any* job—whether it's now, or at any other time in your life—you should always understand your reasons for doing it. Why? Because if you don't understand the root problem that's driving you away, then you'll never be able to solve it—and you may end up repeating the same mistake, over and over again.

To get at the cause of your problem, try doing some brainstorming. Think about what's bothering you, or maybe talk about it with a few friends. Jot down a list of ideas.

When you are ready, you should be able to finish these sentences:

I want to leave my job because _____.

I would like to find a new job that offers

_____.

Fill in the blanks with your own reasons. Why are you leaving? What do you want to find elsewhere? What is making you unhappy?

There may be more than one thing listed in each of your sentences—and that's okay. You may have multiple reasons you are leaving, and multiple things that you are looking for in a new job. Now is the time to list them all down.

By writing down your reasons for leaving and what you want in a new job, you will automatically give your job search more clarity. Now you know exactly what you are looking for, and as you go through interviews and want ads, you'll be more certain that you'll find it.

Of course, once you write down your reasons, you may realize that you actually do not want to change jobs at all. Maybe after writing down your list, you realize that it's a work challenge that you could actually solve with your manager; or maybe it's a situation that you feel will improve over time. That's okay, too.

For example, if your reason for leaving is that you would really like to spend more time with your baby, but right now your job is a full-time, forty-hour-per-week job, then you may be able to ask your manager about moving to four days a week, part-time. If she agrees to it, then you may be able to get it resolved—without the major upheaval of finding a new job.

Remember, starting a new job is a tremendous life change. It comes with a lot of stress. Since you already have a lot of stress going on in your life with a new baby, changing jobs may not be the best choice. Even if your workplace is less than ideal, it may be wiser to wait a few months to get back on your feet before making another major change.

So if you are generally satisfied with your job but have a few complaints that are annoying (but tolerable), try addressing them first with your boss. You may be able to get them resolved, and get what you want—while still keeping your job. If it doesn't work out, then you can always wait a month or two before starting your job search, giving you the opportunity to get stronger, more confident, and more productive (and ultimately giving you a better chance to find a great job).

Here are the top things new moms look for in a new job:

1. **Compensation**—better pay or benefits
2. **Schedule**—a more family-friendly schedule, such as part-time or flex-time
3. **Boredom**—a job that is less routine, less boring
4. **Burnout**—a job that is more interesting, stimulating, or less stressful
5. **Stress**—a job that is less demanding or dangerous
6. **Career advancement**—a job that puts you closer to the career you want
7. **Environment**—a more family-friendly office environment and/or manager
8. **Personal fit**—a job that just simply fits you better personally, perhaps in the same field or industry

What about Starting Your Own Business?

Many new moms that I meet are interested in quitting their jobs to start their own business. They feel that it would be easier to run a business than to work a full-time job while their babies are young. While teaching seminars and coaching hundreds of small businesses, I meet many women who start their businesses for this reason.

While there are definite advantages to being a self-employed mother—including flexibility, more time with your baby, and the ability to take care of doctor visits—there are also many serious downsides that new mothers don't fully consider before starting a business. For example, in that tough first year of business, you will have lots and lots of expenses—possibly thousands of dollars worth—and very little income. It takes at least a year to really build up a business to be strong (and sometimes more). Also, you will probably not have any medical benefits for yourself. And, of course, you will be learning a job. In my case, if I had not already had an established business for more than five years when I delivered Zack, neither the business nor I would have survived.

If you are determined to start a business anyway, I strongly suggest using baby's first year to dream about and plan your business—then save your money from your job to prepare you for that tough first year as an entrepreneur. If you are really ambitious, start your business part-time outside of your work schedule, and see if it's what you really want to do. Once you get enough customers, you can quit your job more comfortably.

Starting a new business is as challenging as having a new baby. If you do both at once, it will be like having twins (and if you already have twins, then it will be like having triplets!). If this sounds exhausting, that's because it is. Consider that doing both at once will put a tremendous strain on your marriage, as well as your finances.

Best Careers for Moms

According to *www.divinecaroline.com*, the best careers for moms are:

1. Writing
2. Teaching
3. "By appointment" jobs (such as career coach)
4. Client services work (such as accounting, bookkeeping, or legal work)
5. Health care jobs
6. Sales jobs

Timing Is Important

No doubt, changing jobs while you are pregnant, nursing, or just a new mom in general will be more challenging than when your infant is at least a year old. Why? Because now is the time when you are already learning a new job—mommy—and it will be challenging to learn yet another new job.

Employers know this. They realize that new mothers are likely to be more focused on their babies than on their careers. And even if you find that you can focus exclusively on your job, with little distraction, your manager will probably still be afraid that you can't. He may see you as a risk.

"Employers can't discriminate against you when they are hiring," says Lynne. "But of course, if you're interviewing when you're eight or nine months along, it's very difficult for some employers to see you with the same eyes as someone who is not pregnant."

However, it's not impossible. April quit her job when her son Ty was only six months old. She says that being straightforward in her interviews helped her set the right expectations with potential employers. "I was honest and confident enough to say to interviewers, 'This is what I have going on with my family, so if that's not workable, then I'm probably not a good fit for your company.'" In the end, April's direct approach helped her find a new job that helped advance her career—while still being family-friendly.

Can it be done? Yes. Will it be more challenging? Probably. If you can get your problem resolved at your current job, then maybe it's worth one more shot before switching employers. If not, then it's time to update your resume.

Conduct Your Job Search on the Sly

Whether you are actively interviewing for a job or just window-shopping, your best bet is to be discreet. There's no reason for your current manager (or anyone else at your job) to know that you are looking for a new one.

Why the secretive approach? Because your manager (or coworkers) may be very hurt, angry, or offended that you are looking for a new job—especially if they've gone out of their way to accommodate your transition to motherhood. And even if your problems with the job seem obvious to you, they may not share your opinion (for example, other employees may feel like the work environment and schedule are perfectly acceptable).

If your manager accidentally discovers you're job searching, she may be caught totally off guard—which will lead to bad feelings. If you ultimately can't find a job, or decide to stop looking, the damage has already been done. Your work environment may be poisoned by the fact that your manager found you looking for a new job, which may actually make your work life worse for you.

Even if you are dead set on finding a new job, remember that lots of things can happen with a job search. You may not find a new job that is better than yours. You may get turned down for the ones that you want. Or somewhere along the line, you may simply decide you'd rather not change jobs—for whatever reason.

The bottom line is that you don't want to screw up your current situation at work with your job search. So for the moment, keep your job search strictly private—no matter how tempted you may be to tell a trusted coworker. Save the job search discussions for your husband or friends outside of work. Inform potential employers that your job search is "confidential" (minimizing the chance that they'll pick up the phone and call your current boss, which is your worst case scenario).

Cover Your Tracks!

Don't job search while at work—no matter how much time (or access to computers) you may have. This means no surfing for job postings, no e-mails to potential employers using your current work e-mail account, no resume writing or printing, and no phone calls on your current work phone. If someone sees what you are doing and reports it to your manager, you will create a very bad situation. Get a private e-mail and cell phone, and save the job searching for off-work hours.

How long should you keep it a secret? Until you have a start date lined up at your next job and you have filled out all of their paperwork. Yes, job offers can get revoked after they are made. Wait as long as absolutely possible before notifying your manager, and then try to give him at least two weeks' notice—the minimum courtesy expected.

Make Sure That New Job Opportunity Is *Really* a Step Up

Sometimes you are so frustrated with your job, you'll do anything to get out of it—including taking a new job that ends up being worse than the old one. Now is not the time for risky job maneuvers.

In a year that is already marked by super-stressful events for yourself, your marriage, and your home life, make sure that if you do take a new job opportunity, that it really *is* a step up.

Don't add to your stress by desperately grasping on to any new job you can, especially one that you'll end up hating.

Take your time. Evaluate *all* parts of the job—not just the one thing that you want. For example, if you want higher pay, and you are offered $2 more per hour (or $2,000 more per year), don't forget to consider the fact that the new job is eighteen miles farther than your old one—which means you'll be spending all of that new raise in gas money. In fact, you may end up ultimately earning *less* than you did at your old job, because it will cost you so much more to get to and from work!

Here are several criteria to consider when comparing your old job to new opportunities:

- Distance from your house
- Total pay (including bonuses)
- Health benefits
- Work environment
- Your manager
- Type of people working there
- Dress code
- Company culture
- Job requirements
- Job responsibilities
- Schedule
- Lunch and breaks
- Vacation and sick time
- Attitude toward families
- Direction of your career

Don't be surprised if your current manager makes a counteroffer once you announce that you are leaving. If they really like your work, they may offer to give you more of something—pay, time off, flextime. If this solves your problem, then you may decide to take it, and that's fine, too. Whichever option fits your life the best is the right decision for you. Just take your time, and don't rush into anything. The choice is yours.

Once you've decided to change jobs, then it's time to set some goals for yourself. What do you really want out of this new job? By taking a few minutes to think through your objectives, you'll save yourself wasted time pursuing job opportunities that don't fit—and ensure that when you do finally get an offer, the job is just right for you.

After all, job-hunting is an important job—all by itself. To find the best possible job fit for you, you'll need to take it as seriously as any important career move, such as a raise or a promotion.

Make a List of What You Want

To really know what you are looking for, it's best to make an actual list of what you want from your next job. This will help keep you focused through the long hours of looking through job ads, editing your resume, and interviewing with prospective employers.

How do you do this? Easy. Write down everything that you want in your next job. Your list might include your personal preferences on:

- Pay
- Benefits
- Location
- Schedule
- Start date
- Dress code
- Industry
- Field
- Job title
- Total hours
- Coworkers
- Long-term career goals

For example, your list might look like this:

- Casual workplace
- Full medical and dental benefits
- Small company
- Forty hours per week (minimum)
- Within twenty miles from my home
- In the manufacturing industry
- Same job level (floor supervisor)

Next, prioritize your items in order of "most important" to "least important" by adding numbers to them. What is most important to you on this list that you feel you simply must have in your next job? Put a number 1 next to it. For the second most important item, put a 2 next to it . . . and so on.

After you are done prioritizing your items, reorder your list so that number one is at the top. Now, your sample list looks like this:

1. Same job level (floor supervisor)
2. Forty hours per week (minimum)
3. Full medical and dental benefits
4. Within twenty miles from my home
5. Casual workplace
6. Small company
7. In the manufacturing industry

By looking at this list, you can easily see that the most important things to this person are that she stay in the same job level (as a floor supervisor) and that she can get at least forty hours per week. She would probably be more willing to compromise on location and industry than on these two items.

This brings up the point that realistically, you may not be able to get all the things you want in one job. You may have to compromise on some things. By ordering your list in terms of priority, you'll have an easier (and less emotional) time making a decision about your job offers. You can simply look at your list and make sure that you get your top two or three items, at a minimum. The more items you can get from the top of your list, the happier you will be long term with your job.

Which brings us to our next question . . .

How Desperate Are You?

Face it, ladies, sometimes we all just need a little cash. And if that's the case, then you just may need to take the next job you are offered. Ask yourself, "How desperate am I to take a job?"

If the answer is "very desperate," then you may not even care about your first two or three items. You may just want to get the quickest job offer you can. But even here, be wary about taking a job that's a really bad fit for you. After all, then you'll just be out looking for a job again within a few months.

If you have a lot of prospects out there and can hold out for another week or two, then you might at least wait for the second job offer you get. You may actually get more of what you want with job offer number two.

If you already have a job right now, then you can afford to be pickier. In that case, you probably shouldn't take any job that doesn't meet at least your top three requirements—and maybe more.

So, now is the time to take a gut check. Ask yourself how desperate you are to get into a new job. You may know the answer immediately. Or you may need to sleep on it for a few days.

In the meantime, if you get a job offer, politely thank the interviewer and ask him for a day or two to think it over. In fact, no matter *how* excited you are about a job opportunity, you should always take a day or two to think it over—you don't want to rush into anything you may end up hating later.

If it helps, talk it over with a friend. And, of course, discuss it with your partner. After all, he will be affected by your decision, too.

In the end, of course, you have the final decision. If you can't get your top three wishes on your list, but you really need cash immediately and are driving up increasing debt, then maybe you just need to take the job. That's okay, too. It's only temporary, after all.

Consider Your Long-Term Career Objectives

Of course, the other thing to consider is your long-term career goal. Where do you want to be working in five years? And would you be willing to compromise (or lower your expectations on) your top three preferences if it would help you to get closer to that goal?

To help clarify this long-term goal for you, it helps to write it down. Once again, take out your piece of paper, and finish this sentence:

I would like to be _____ by _____.

For example, you might say:

I would like to be *an elementary school art teacher* by *the year 2015*.

Once you have clarified your goal, you can now measure each job offer against it. Post your goal on your desk. For every job offer, ask yourself: "Will this job get me *closer to*—or *farther away from*—my goal?"

Of course, finances (and other factors) may still play a role in your final decision. The wisest choice to meet your current needs may actually be a retreat from your long-term career goal.

But no matter what you choose, remember that it's only temporary—just focus on the first year after the baby's birth and take it one step at a time.

Job-Hunting Challenges for New Moms

When you looked for your last job, it was pretty straightforward: The only person you had to worry about was you. Now, you have a little baby to take care of—and a partner who may be very concerned about your decision, which makes things just a bit more complicated (but still achievable).

Before you begin your job hunt, take a minute to think through a few of the issues involved. Here are the key challenges to finding a new job for a new mother.

Scheduling Interviews

Whether you are working full-time right now, or are at home full-time, it will be difficult to schedule job interviews. So what do you do?

No matter what your situation, you will definitely need to find child care to watch your baby while you are interviewing. No matter how desperate you are, *do not bring your baby to the interview.* It is better to call and reschedule with the interviewer than to bring your baby to the interview.

Why? Because a baby is highly disruptive to business meetings, and it shows disrespect to your potential employer. It will be nearly impossible to focus your attention on the interviewer when your baby is crying, pooping, or spitting up.

Not only that, but any sane interviewer will immediately question the commitment of a prospective employee who brings a child to the interview. It begs the question: "If she can't find child care for a thirty-minute interview, how is she going to be able to come to work every day?" It naturally gives the appearance that you will be more focused on your baby than on your job.

The solution is to find two or three babysitters to be on call while you schedule appointments for job interviews. It's not forever—just for the few weeks (or months) till you find a job.

If you are working a full-time job right now, this may be easier for you, because you may be able to leverage your current child care provider to help out for an extra hour in the morning or evening, before or after your normal work schedule. You may also be able to squeeze in your interviews during your lunch hour or an afternoon off. If you do need extra child care time, be sure to notify your childcare provider as far in advance as possible to make sure there are no conflicts.

Plan Extra Time to Get Ready

When you plan for your interview, remember that you now have a whole little other person to get ready, too—and it always takes longer than you think. You don't want to be late to an interview with a prospective company that you really like, so plan at least *one extra hour* (in *addition* to your normal interview prep time) to get baby dressed, changed, and ready; pack all her stuff; get her in the car; and deliver her to the babysitter. You'll feel less rushed and more confident for your interview.

However, if you are job searching while at home as a full-time mom, then it may be a little trickier. Find two or three babysitters you can work with to schedule interviews. Try family members, friends, neighbors, or even local day care facilities that might be willing to help out. Tell them you are interviewing for a job, and ask them if they can help out by watching your baby periodically for two hours while you go in for the interviews. Let them know it could be on short notice and ask them which days and times would work best for them.

Once you are ready to schedule your interview, get a few available times from the interviewer, then call your babysitters to find out who is available. Pick a time, then book both the babysitter and the interviewer.

Of course, you need to pay your babysitters, just like anyone else—even if it's just family and friends. After all, you're taking up their time, too. While it may cost you a few dollars, consider it an investment in your future career.

Another option is to dedicate one day per week to your job search—and find a regular child care provider for that time. You can work on resumes, search want ads, and schedule all of your interviews on that day. This will streamline your child care situation, and make it easier for you. The downside is that you may not be able to get all of your interviews scheduled for a single day per week—but you can try.

Finally, don't forget about asking your partner. Even if it means rearranging the schedule for his job, or taking a little time off, it may be worth it to him. After all, two incomes are better than one!

Where Can You Find Maternity Clothes Appropriate for an Interview?

While you may be in between your pre- and post-baby sizes, it is important that you find an outfit that fits you well now—even if it means buying a new interview outfit that you may only wear one or two times. If you are lucky, you may have a privately owned maternity boutique in your town. If so, start there. If not, try a national chain store that carries business maternity clothes that will fit you both before and after delivery such as Target, Old Navy, Kohl's, or Mimi Maternity.

Encountering Discrimination

Although it still happens occasionally, discrimination is wrong. "Employers can't discriminate against you in any way for being pregnant," says Lynne. "That is illegal in this country."

Further, a prospective employer cannot ask you about your motherhood status. Interviewers should not ask any questions about your pregnancy, including if you're going to need time off.

You may, however, voluntarily disclose information about your pregnancy. If you are obviously pregnant, then that may be the best thing for you to do. But you certainly aren't required to do it.

Of course, discrimination sometimes happens anyway. If you feel you've been discriminated against, you have a couple of options for handling it: Take legal action, or ignore it and move on to a better company.

Most women do the latter. After all, if the company is biased against you during their *interview* process, what will they be like to actually *work* for? It's probably not going to be very pleasant. In that case, thank them graciously for the interview and move on to a better company that will appreciate you—and treat you as an asset.

Negotiating the New Position

Once you've found the right job, you're ready to negotiate for what you want in your new position. Don't be shy about asking for what you need.

Know Your Value

Are you an asset to this new company? Absolutely. But you'll never get them to see it if you don't believe it yourself. The best way you can help yourself negotiate for what you want in the new position is to know your value. If you have confidence in yourself as an asset to any organization, then you are more likely to get what you want.

Not sure how to define your value? Afraid that you come with too many negatives as a new mom? Then it's time to make a list. What aspects of your work talents and accomplishments would a new employer appreciate?

Jot down all of the things that are valuable about you as an employee. Be generous. What do you bring to the table? Note anything and everything that comes to mind. Think of your:

- Education
- Experiences
- Achievements
- Abilities
- Contributions to past jobs

For example, maybe you are really good working under deadlines and you are an excellent team player. Or maybe you consistently produced the highest-quality product at your last job. Maybe you are a reliable person, who shows up day after day. Or perhaps you outperformed your entire office two years in a row in sales. Whatever is unique about you, put it in your list. Try to come up with at least five things that are valuable about your work experience.

When you are done, reread the list. Do you see your value? I hope so. You are a fabulous employee! And you're worth every penny.

Keep this list, and reread it before every interview or negotiation. By treating yourself as an asset, you gain confidence in your abilities—and look more attractive to employers.

Ask for What You Want

To really get what you want in your new job—whether it's a higher salary, a flexible schedule, or a higher-level position—you have to ask for it. If you don't ask, you won't have a chance.

But before you ask, learn as much as you can about the company, the job, and the industry. "Really do your research—and find out as much as you can," Lynne recommends. "Educate yourself about what salaries are standard at this company, or in your field. See if you can find out what is offered to others at the company. Make sure you are getting a fair shake."

This means asking the interviewer lots of questions about the job itself. It also means spending some time on the Internet beforehand, learning about the company and what they do. You may also want to look at compensation studies in your field if you can find them (and remember to make allowances for your geographic region—some cities pay more than others due to local conditions). Read any magazine or newspaper articles you can find about the company and its industry. Talk to other people at the company, if possible, to find out whatever you can about the culture, benefits, and work environment.

Once you know as much as possible about the job, the company, and the industry, you will be in a better position to ask for what you want—and you'll know whether your requests are reasonable. For example, if you learn that everyone else in your job title at this same company starts at $40,000/year, then you know that you are asking for too little if you request a starting salary of $35,000/year.

Finally, ask for what you want. You know your value. If you want $42,000/year instead, your first step is to ask—but you also have to communicate your value to your prospective new manager. Communicate what you want—and also what you will bring to the company.

CHAPTER 17

What If You Decide to Stay Home?

So, you were all set to go back to work after your baby arrived. You were even ready to leap ahead in your career. But instead, you brought that baby home and fell in love. And you can't imagine going back to work. Now what?

If it happens to you, don't worry. It happens to lots of new moms. Here are a few things to consider before making your final decision.

Don't Be Hasty

Don't be in a rush right now to make a decision about your job—especially not before your maternity leave is over. Even if you feel a burning desire, wait to make your decision for at least one or two months after you go back to work. Many women have been 100 percent sure they want to stay home, only to find themselves missing the challenge of work as their babies grow older and less dependent.

Remember, you can always quit later—you still have the option. But waiting gives you some time to ride out the emotional first weeks after baby arrives, when your hormones are still raging and you may even be experiencing some postpartum depression. Waiting until you're back at work a few months will ensure that you make the best possible decision.

Evaluate All the Factors

Before you make your final decision, be sure to evaluate all the factors involved. You will also want to discuss them fully with your partner first. By evaluating a list of criteria methodically, you will be less likely to make an overly emotional decision that you'll regret later.

Ask yourself the following questions:

- Will I enjoy staying home with the baby full-time?
- Will I miss my work?
- Does this fulfill a dream for me?
- Can I afford to quit?
- Will we still be able to pay our bills and expenses if I do quit?
- Will I feel understimulated if I stay at home?
- How will this impact my long-term career goals?
- What will I sacrifice to do this?
- Am I willing to put my career goals on hold for a while?

Even if you evaluate all the factors, however, the bottom line is that you won't really know whether you're going to enjoy being a stay-at-home mom until you try it. While this may seem scary, lots of working moms try it at some point in their careers. After all, full-time motherhood may be an important personal dream for you to explore—and one that you'll regret later if you miss out. For that reason alone, it may be worth the effort.

Talk to Your Partner!

You cannot make this decision without your partner's support. Make sure he's involved as early in your decision process as possible. After all, he is 50 percent of this partnership. No matter how emotional you feel about this issue, be sure to listen to his input and acknowledge it.

Besides, if you play your cards right, you may be able to come back to your same job later (see the section titled "Don't Burn Bridges" later in this same chapter). And if that doesn't work out, you are smart enough—and capable enough—to find another job.

Consider Alternatives to Quitting

Of course, it doesn't have to be one thing or the other—full-time work versus full-time mommy. If you are still uncertain, why not try negotiating a work schedule at your current job that gives you more time with your baby?

Many companies now offer:

- Part-time
- Flextime
- Job sharing
- Telecommuting

And even if your company doesn't *officially* offer these options, they may still do it for you if you ask—especially if you are a stellar employee that they want to retain. (For more on alternate work arrangements, see Chapter 3, Negotiating a New Work Schedule.)

Don't Burn Bridges

No matter how unhappy you feel about your boss or your job, don't burn any bridges when you leave. Be as polite, thankful, and considerate as you possibly can with your departure.

You never know when you might want to come back to the same company, or when your boss might land at a different company. You could end up back in the same industry, and they could become a customer of yours later—or vice-versa.

Lynne recommends being courteous at all costs. "Always take the high road—don't trash your boss or company on the way out," she says. "Don't blame them, don't get on a website and blog about them. Don't do any of that."

Tell your boss first about your decision. Don't let her hear it as gossip from other employees, which will only make her feel angry. And while you are meeting with her, tell her how much you appreciate all she's done for you. Give her a small gift or thank you card. As Lynne points out, "Being gracious will always serve you."

Be aware that no matter which way you go, there will always be challenges. Even if your dream is to ultimately be a full-time stay-at-home mom, there are challenges there, too. While your son or daughter will get the best care possible, you may still miss socializing with other adults. It will be difficult to get time for yourself, and it can be boring. You may also miss the stimulation and achievement of work that you have become accustomed to.

So don't worry about whether you are making the right decision. If you decide to stay at home for the moment, you can always change your mind later. There are plenty of jobs out there! Think of it this way: It's not permanent—it's just another step in the incredible lifetime journey of being a working mother.

A Final Note to You, the Working Mother

In the end, there are no right—or wrong—ways to handle the challenges of being a working mother. While I've given you lots of ideas throughout this book, only *you* can decide what's right for you and your baby. So consider these ideas to be suggestions only. After all, you may come up with even more creative solutions yourself!

One thing I know for certain: New things will come up for you every day that you have never faced before. Some of those things will be exciting, like your child's first tooth. Some of those things will be scary, like the new arguments you'll have with your partner.

I wish I could tell you that it will all be fluffy, pink, and happy. Of course, some of it will! (Especially if you have a girl!) But much of it won't. It will also be messy, poopy, frustrating, and sometimes boring. There will be as many laughs (for both you and baby) as tears in that first year.

The good news is that the first four months are the toughest. If you can make it through those, you'll survive. When I called my good friend in tears six weeks after my baby was born (right after I returned to work), she told me, "Circle the day on your calendar four months after your baby was born. I promise you, life will get better on that day." She was right.

Of course, you are not alone. There are millions of other working moms out there—many of them doing it solo. If you are really stuck with a problem, reach out to one of them and ask her how she handled it. The mommy network that you call for help will prove to be an invaluable resource—whether it's about teething pain, late-night feedings, or dishes that are so crusted with food they are moldy and utterly unwashable.

So as you face new challenges as a mother—related to work or otherwise—then reach out to someone. Call, e-mail, or visit a mommy friend today. Ask her how she did it. There's a solution to every problem. And remember: Yes, you *can* do this.

If you happen to stumble on a new idea for handling these challenges, I'd love to hear from you. Please visit me at *www .paulapeters.com* and tell me what you think. I look forward to hearing your wonderful new ideas!

Go get 'em, mom!

Resources

Associated Press. "100 Best Companies for Working Mothers, According to *Working Mother* Magazine." *USA Today*, September 25, 2006, *www.usatoday.com/money/workplace/2006-09-25-working-momschart_x.htm*.

Downs, Barbara. "Fertility of American Women: June 2002." U.S. Census Bureau, October 2003.

Doyle, Rodger. "Breaking the Mold: A Real Family Value: Mothers Who Work Outside the Home." *Scientific American*, March 2007, p. 32.

"Facts for Features: Mother's Day May 14, 2006." U.S. Census Bureau, March 15, 2006, *www.census.gov/Press-Release/www/releases/archives*.

Gottman, John, and Julie Schwartz Gottman. *And Baby Makes Three: The Six-Step Plan for Preserving Marital Intimacy and Rekindling Romance after Baby Arrives*. New York: Crown Publishers, 2007.

Hayghe, Howard. "Working Mothers Reach Record Number in 1984." *Monthly Labor Review*, December 1984, pp. 31–34.

Johnson, Julia Overturf, and Barbara Downs. "Maternity Leave and Employment Patterns of First-Time Mothers: 1961–2000." U.S. Census Bureau, October 2005.

Joyce, Amy. "Developing Boomerang Mothers: Some Companies Set Up Maternity-Leave Programs with an Emphasis on the Return." *Washington Post*, March 11, 2007, *www.washingtonpost.com*.

Kantor, Jodi. "On the Job, Nursing Mothers Find a 2-Class System." *New York Times*, August 28, 2007, *www.nytimes.com*.

Lerner, Sharon. "The Motherhood Experiment." *New York Times*, March 4, 2007, p. 20.

Loeb, Marshall. "Five Ways New Moms Can Protect Their Jobs." *Wall Street Journal*, November 15, 2007, *www.careerjournal.com*.

McKay, Dawn Rosenberg. "6 Reasons to Make a Career Change." 2007. *www.about.com.*

Munoz, Sara Schaefer. "Making a Case for New Moms to Remain in the Work Force." *Wall Street Journal,* The Juggle Blog, *www.wsj.com/thejuggle.*

"Parents and the High Price of Child Care: 2007 Update." National Association of Child Care Resource & Referral Agencies, *www.naccrra.org/news/pricereport.php.*

Reistad-Long, Sara. "8 Ways to Get Back in the Game after the Mommy Years." *O Magazine,* September 2007, pp. 233–34.

Rosen, Ruth. "The Care Crisis: How Women Are Bearing the Burden of a National Emergency." *Nation,* March 12, 2007, pp. 11–16.

Shellenbarger, Sue. "Trading Carpools for Cubicles: More Moms Return to Work." *Wall Street Journal,* August 2007, *www.careerjournal.com.*

Shuman, Tracy C., editor. "Understanding Labor and Delivery Complications—the Basics." WebMD, August 1, 2005, *www.webmd.com.*

Smith, Kristin, Barbara Downs, and Martin O'Connell. "Maternity Leave and Employment Patterns: 1961–1995." U.S. Census Bureau, November 2001.

U.S. Department of Labor. "Family and Medical Leave Act Advisor: Frequently Asked Questions and Answers." *www.dol.gov/elaws/esa/fmla/faq.asp.*

U.S. Department of Labor, Employment Standards Administration. "The Family and Medical Leave Act of 1993." February 5, 1993, *www.dol.gov/esa/whd/regs/statutes/fmla.htm.*

Wilbert, Caroline. "The Six Best Careers for Moms." January, 2008. *www.divinecaroline.com.*

Index

Aitchison, Will, 27
Alpert, Barbara, 137
Alternate work arrangements, 36–41, 203
And Baby Makes Three, 150, 156
Au pair, 70–71

Babysitters, 69, 74, 77, 165, 180, 196–97. *See also* Child care
Back-to-work trick, 98–99
Bennett, Shoshana S., 163
Best careers, 188
Best companies, 183
The Best 30-Minute Recipe, 137
Bodian, Stephan, 167
Boss
    communicating with, 26
    reconnecting with, 90–91
    sharing plans with, 53–55
    and sick time, 117–20
Breastfeeding
    benefits of, 102–3
    choosing, 103–4
    negotiating, 107–8
    and weight loss, 173–74
    and work, 101–8
Breast pump, 104–6
Burgoyne, John, 137
Burning bridges, 204
Business startup, 187. *See also* Self-employment
Busy People's Super Simple 30-Minute Menus, 137

Career goals, 94–99, 194–95
Career plan, creating, 47–50, 184–86
Career plan, defining, 45–47
Catching up at work, 89–99
Changing jobs, 183–200
Child care
    choosing, 77–79
    costs of, 64
    guilt about, 64–65
    interviews for, 76–77
    options for, 65–73
    planning, 63–80

schedule for, 79–80
searching for, 73–80
and self-employment, 59, 61
for sick baby, 117
Chores
    cooking meals, 135–40
    daily planner for, 143–46
    help with, 131–34, 176–80
    house-cleaning tips, 129–31
    meal-planning tips, 134–35
    minimizing, 125–34
Clothing options, 169, 174, 197
Codey, Mary Jo, 163
Company policies, 28–29, 41–42. *See also* Family and Medical Leave Act
Complications with baby, 31, 111, 113–14
Conflict, handling, 156–58
Conflict, and emotions, 155–58
Continuing to work, 11–23, 56–57
Cookbooks, 136–37
Cooking tips, 135–40
Counselors, 133, 157–58
Coworkers, communicating with, 55–58, 92, 97, 99, 108
Customers, losing, 60–61

Dads, 29, 150–51, 165, 178
Daily planner, 143–46
Daily responsibilities, 143–47
Davich, Victor, 167
Day care, 63–80. *See also* Child care
Decision-making tips, 20–22, 201–4
Depression, 86–87, 162–63
Diet, 170–72
Dining out, 135
Dinners
    cookbooks for, 136–37
    cooking, 135–40
    freezing, 139–40
    planning, 134–35
Dinnertime expectations, 135–36
Dinnertime tips, 135–40
Discrimination, 198
Doctor appointments, 109–20
Doctor duty, 116–17

Eight Minute Meditation: Quiet Your Mind, Change Your Life, 167
Eisaguirre, Lynne, 3, 29
Emotions
    and child care, 64–65
    and conflict, 155–58
    and postpartum depression, 86–87, 162–63
    understanding, 19–20, 83–87
Encouragement, 205–6
Enjoyment of work, 17–18
Exercise, 170–72
Expectations, 60, 135–36, 167–70
Expenses, 13–14, 64

Family and Medical Leave Act (FMLA), 25–32, 119
Family assistance, 15–16
Fathers, 29, 150–51, 165, 178
Fatigue
    alleviating, 165–68, 176
    causes of, 86, 161–65
    understanding, 161–68
Feeling left out, 150–51
Feelings, 16–19, 21, 83–87. *See also* Emotions
Financial considerations, 12–16, 64, 203
Flextime, 37–38, 203
The FMLA: Understanding the Family and Medical Leave Act, 27
Food diary, 170–71
Freezing meals, 139–40

Girlfriend-time, 20, 182
Goals for work, 94–99, 194–95
Gottfried, Adele E., 19
Gottfried, Allen W., 19
Gottman, John M., 150, 156
Gottman, Julie Schwartz, 150, 156
Guests at home, 131
Guilt, 19–20, 64–65, 83

Hall, Dawn, 137
Health concerns, 109–20, 161–74
Health insurance, 110, 114–15, 157

Hiring help, 133–34, 180
Hospital day care, 71–72
House-cleaning tips, 129–31
Household chores, 125–40. *See also* Chores
Household responsibilities, 123–40

Immunizations, 112
Income, 13–14, 200
In-home day care, 66–67
Insurance, 114–15
Interview tips, 195–98
Irwin, Dena, 137

Jasper, Margaret, 27
Job. *See also* Work
    catching up at, 89–99
    changes at, 92–93
    changing, 183–200
    continuing with, 11–23, 56–57
    enjoyment of, 17–18
    interviews for, 195–98
    juggling, 141–48
    opportunities for, 189–91
    preferences for, 191–94
    pros and cons of, 20–21, 201–4
    quitting, 11–23, 201–4
    returning to, 89–90, 98–99
    schedules, 33–43, 147–48
    searching for, 188–89, 195–98
    sharing, 40, 203
Journaling, 19, 21, 170–71
Juggling jobs and family, 141–48

Kleiman, Karen, 163

Lactation room, 105
Lang, Diana, 167
Legal issues, 25–32, 119
LeMasters, E. E., 149
Loss of interest, 87, 162
Lund, JoAnna M., 137

Manager
    communicating with, 26
    reconnecting with, 90–91

sharing plans with, 53–55
and sick time, 117–20
Maternity clothes, 169, 174, 197
Maternity leave, planning, 51–61
Maternity leave, understanding, 25–32
McCloskey, Suzanne, 163
Meal planning, 134–35
Medical benefits, 17–18
Medical insurance, 110, 114–15, 157
Meditation, 166–67
Meditation for Dummies, 167
Missing baby, 83–87
Mommy time, 152, 175–82
Mood swings, 87, 162
Morgan, Jeff, 137
Morgan, Jodie, 137
*The Mother-to-Mother Postpartum
Depression Support Book*, 163
Myths, 19

Nannies, 69–70, 75–77
Negotiating breastfeeding, 107–8
Negotiating maternity leave, 30
Negotiating work schedules, 33–43
New job, 198–200. *See also* Job
New responsibilities, 151–53
New schedule, negotiating, 41–43
Night feedings, 143, 150, 163, 165, 168
Nissenberg, Sandra K., 137
Nursing baby, 101–8. *See also*
Breastfeeding

O'Neil-Hill, Lindsey, 5, 67
*Opening to Meditation: A Gentle, Guided
Approach*, 167

Panel of working moms, 2–8
Part-time work, 36–37, 203
Paternity leave, 29
Pediatrician appointments, 109, 112–13
Personal choices, 30
Personal values, 29–30
Planning ahead, 142–48
Planning child care, 63–80
Planning maternity leave, 25–32,
51–61

Planning meals, 134–35
Planning workweek, 143–48
"Plan of attack," 94–99
Postpartum checkups, 110–11. *See also*
Doctor appointments
Postpartum depression, 86–87, 162–63
Postpartum Depression Demystified, 163
Postpartum Depression for Dummies, 163
Poulin, Sandra, 163
Prioritizing, 92–93, 96–97, 124–25,
192–93
Professional help, 157–58
Pros and cons of working, 20–21,
201–4

*Quick Meals for Healthy Kids and Busy
Parents*, 137
Quitting work, 11–23, 201–4

Raskin, Valerie, 163
Ray, Rachael, 137
Reducing chores, 127–29
Reducing travel time, 40
Relationship tips, 149–58
Relaxation time, 152, 176–77, 180–82
Resources, 207–8
Responsibilities, daily, 123–47. *See also*
Chores
Responsibilities, new, 151–53
Returning to work, 89–90, 98–99
Romance, lack of, 153–55

Salaries, 200
Schedules, negotiating, 33–43
Schedules, re-evaluating, 147–48
Seasonal work, 39
Self-employment, 31, 58–61, 114–15,
187
Sex, lack of, 153–55
Sick baby, and day care, 117
Sick baby, and doctor appointments,
112–13
Sick time-off, 116–20
Single moms, 15–16, 117, 132–33, 143
Sleep patterns, 163–65
Special care, 113–14

Stamina, 94–95, 98
Starting new business, 187
State agencies, 16, 72–73
State-sponsored day care, 72–73
Staying home, 201–4
Stress at home, 18
Stress on relationship, 149–58
Stuppy, Dr. Kristen K., 4, 38
Suicidal thoughts, 87, 162
Sullivan, Dr. Teri, 2, 15

Take-out food, 135
Telecommuting, 38–39, 203
Temporary work, 39
Therapists, 157–58
Thirty-Minute Meals, 137
Thirty Minutes to Mealtime, 137
This Isn't What I Expected: Overcoming
    Postpartum Depression, 163
Threesome, 149–50
Time for self, 152, 175–82
Travel, 40, 107
Two-income families, 141–48
Twosome, 149–50

Unique solutions, 36–41, 203

Venis, Joyce A., 163
Visitors at home, 131

The Weeknight Survival Cookbook, 137
Weight loss, 168–74
Well-baby appointments, 17, 109,
    112–13, 116, 118–19
Work. See also Job
    catching up at, 89–99
    changes at, 92–93
    continuing with, 11–23, 56–57
    enjoyment of, 17–18
    interviews for, 195–98
    juggling, 141–48
    opportunities for, 189–91
    preferences for, 191–94
    pros and cons of, 20–21, 201–4
    quitting, 11–23, 201–4
    returning to, 89–90, 98–99

schedules, 33–43, 147–48
searching for, 188–89, 195–98
Working moms panel, 2–8
Working mothers myth, 19
Working Mother 100 Best Companies,
    183
The Working Parents Cookbook, 137
Workplace day care, 68–69
Work schedules, negotiating, 33–43
Work schedules, re-evaluating, 147–48
Workweek, planning, 143–48
Workweek, re-evaluating, 147–48
Writing in journal, 19, 21, 170–71

Your Rights under the FMLA, 27

About the Author

Photo by Mark Havran

Paula Peters is an accomplished working mother, author, business owner, speaker, and trainer who has delivered seminars to thousands of people throughout North America. She is the author of *The Ultimate Marketing Toolkit* and *The Quick-and-Easy Web Site*. In addition, Paula has published more than fifty articles, essays, and short stories nationwide and has been the recipient of two awards for her work. She lives with her husband and son in the Kansas City area.

To learn more, or to contact the author, please visit *www.paulapeters.com* or *www.peterswriting.com*. She is also available for speaking engagements and writing projects for your organization.